Not that Man!

Nicholas King is a Jesuit priest who teaches New Testament at Oxford University. He is fond of playing squash and cricket. He is frequently in demand to lecture on biblical subjects, especially St Paul.

Not that Man!

Restoring St Paul's reputation

Nicholas King

Acclaimed translator of the Bible

Augsburg Books
MINNEAPOLIS

NOT THAT MAN!
Restoring St Paul's reputation

© Copyright 2009 Nicholas King.
Original edition published in English under the title NOT THAT MAN!
by Kevin Mayhew Ltd, Buxhall, England.

This edition published in 2020 by Fortress Press. All rights reserved. Except for brief quotations in critical articles or reviews, no part of this book may be reproduced in any manner without prior written permission from the publisher. Email copyright@augsburgfortress.org or write to Permissions, Fortress Press, PO Box 1209, Minneapolis, MN 55440-1209.

Cover image: Emily Drake
Cover design: Emily Drake

Print ISBN: 978-1-5064-6009-3

Contents

Introduction	7
1. What changed Paul?	11
2. What did Paul write, and how?	35
3. Did Paul think that Jesus was God?	53
4. What did Jesus do for us?	71
5. Paul on building the Christian community	89
6. Paul on prayer	123
7. Paul on preaching	137
8. Paul on Church leadership	155
9. Paul and the outside world	169
10. Paul and slavery	185
11. Paul and women	207
12. Paul and sex	235
Conclusion	249
Suggestions for further reading	251

*For the Jesuits of the South African Region,
in gratitude*

Introduction

The year from 28 June 2008 to 29 June 2009 was declared by Pope Benedict XVI, in the presence of representatives from other churches, to be the 'Year of St Paul'. It has turned out to be quite a year, with Pauline scholars being summoned here, there and everywhere to share their thoughts on the Apostle of the Gentiles. What follows is a distillation of some lectures given, mainly to Catholic priests and other ministers, in four different venues in South Africa in July and August 2008. It was an extraordinary experience to be back in that strange and yet familiar country, and to be sharing my jejune insights on Paul's writings. One of the remarks I heard most often was, 'I thought that I didn't like St Paul – but now I have to think it through again', and that has encouraged me to put the lectures down on paper.

The shape of the book may need some explanation. Lectures, particularly where there is interaction between lecturer and audience, do not easily lend themselves to the printed format. Roughly what happened was that the heavier lectures were given in the morning, when people were at their freshest; and those are the first six chapters of this book. In the afternoon, it was felt better to give something a bit lighter, after all that hard work, and that is what you will find in the next three chapters. The final three chapters were originally talks aimed at a wider audience, and so they have titles that are more 'exciting'. The result is that this book should get easier to read as you go on, and that may be a good thing.

As you read the book, you will notice a certain amount of repetition. There are key passages to which I shall return more than once. This is not intended to bore you, but may serve to underscore the fact that Paul is someone whom you have to keep revisiting, from several different angles, if you are to go deeper into the mystery of this extraordinary character.

Many people think that they dislike St Paul, and this book is for them. The title was originally to have been 'St Paul: for those who hate St Paul'; it was not intended to upset anybody, least of all St Paul, and was based on the suggestion, made long ago, of my brother Michael. It was based on an LP record (for those of us who are old enough to remember LP records) that we had in our house as children, called *Classical Music for Those Who Hate Classical Music*. However, it has been decided that this was rather too strong medicine. The new title is *Not That Man!* (for reasons that will become clear in Chapter Eleven), but I should still like to offer Michael my affectionate gratitude.

A different kind of thanks is due to all those who hosted me in South Africa, especially, but not exclusively, my brother-Jesuits, who looked after me so very well. Peter Dainty has been the copy-editor of unceasing vigilance for this book; as always, it has been a very great pleasure to work with him, and I have learnt a great deal in the process. I would also like to thank Alison Evans who dealt so graciously with my eccentricities. Joanna Clark, undergraduate at Worcester College, Oxford, who never failed to brighten our tutorials on St Paul with her perceptiveness and sense of humour, has read every word of the manuscript and made some very helpful suggestions. To them, and to many others here unnamed, I owe a very great debt of gratitude. It would be nice to blame them for the mistakes in this book, but honesty compels me to admit that all the errors are my own.

It seemed important to quote extensively from the text of Paul, to illustrate the points being made, and to bring out the freshness that Paul pours forth in all his writing. The translations are always my own; they do not however in every case coincide with the version that you will find in *The New Testament, freshly translated* (Kevin Mayhew, 2004). You are encouraged to refer also to that volume, and indeed to some other translation, to make sure that I am not pulling a fast one. Translations from the Old Testament are also my own; generally I have taken them from the Hebrew (MT), except where it was important to take it from the Greek (LXX) which was what Paul had at his fingertips. And when you see a reference to Paul or some other scriptural author, may I ask you to look it up, in a Bible kept handy for the purpose? It will both enable you to check up on what is written here, and help you to get to know Paul better. Which is what this book is all about.

NICHOLAS KING SJ

One

What changed Paul?

Introduction

There are many reasons for not liking St Paul. He is, we have to admit, authoritarian; he can be prickly and defensive. He can also be downright obscure; if you have read the Letter to the Romans and thought that you understood it all, then look again, and you will discover that you were reading in too much of a hurry. Then there are those (though as you will see in a later chapter, I am not one of them) who regard Paul as somewhat misogynistic.

There are on the other hand many reasons for quite liking him. In the first place, Paul is a translator. He takes the message of Jesus – and the message about Jesus that Jesus' first disciples proclaimed in the Galilean Aramaic that was their dialect, filled as it was with images of rural Palestine – and translated it into the Greek that was spoken in the Hellenistic cities where Paul was most at home. That was a decisive move in setting the gospel free to be proclaimed throughout the Roman Empire, where Greek was the language of political and economic discourse, rather as English is today (and, for all I know, Mandarin Chinese tomorrow).

Secondly, Paul is a brilliant theologian, one of the three great minds in the New Testament. The other two are the author of the Fourth Gospel and the author of that astonishing text, the Letter to the Hebrews (and, for at least some shrewd observers, a fourth would be the author of the Gospel of Mark); but perhaps Paul is the greatest, for he has a few basic principles, which we shall be talking about in this chapter, and then he has to think on his feet. We can often feel him doing just that, as he responds to different needs in the churches that he has founded.

Thirdly, Paul is a passionate lover, and 'all the world loves a lover'. Something happened to Paul (this is the answer to our question, what changed Paul?) and he fell in love with Jesus, and with the people to whom Jesus directed him. That is an aspect of Paul that we should never neglect, for it is the key to his undeniably difficult writings.

Lastly (and you may not feel that this is a reason for liking him) you never quite have Paul pinned down. Just when you think you have understood him, he goes laughing away from you, and you realise that you have to think again. So whenever this book gives the impression of having 'caught' Paul, then be prepared to think that it may have got him wrong.

Where Paul came from

We do not well understand Paul unless we realise that there were three formative elements in his background. Each of them was important to him, but he had his reservations about them all. In the first place, he was a Jew, properly brought up as a Pharisee. If Luke has it right (see Acts 22:3), he was given his religious training in Jerusalem, so he had seen Herod's spectacular and beautiful reordering of the Second Temple, and knew the Pharisees intimately (Philippians 3:5), the party within Judaism that was to take on the mantle of leadership after that Temple was destroyed (some years after Paul's own death). Paul was very much a Jew, though he also had his disagreements with his fellow Jews.

Secondly, he was a product of Greek culture. He may well have known Aramaic and Hebrew (one would rather expect that to be the case); but when you read his letters it is clear that here is one who handles Greek with the skill and originality of a native speaker. Many scholars today will argue that Paul had at least some training in Greek rhetorical techniques. So he was a man who, precisely as Luke depicts him in Acts 17 (the speech to the Areopagus), is entirely at his ease in the dazzling Greek-speaking society that inhabited the principal cities of the Mediterranean world, though he undoubtedly had reservations about some elements of that Hellenistic society, as indeed he did about the Judaism on which he had been brought up.

Thirdly, Paul was a Roman citizen. Paul knew how to use the infrastructure of the Empire, its postal and travel services; and both Acts and Romans represent Paul as determined to get to Rome. Indeed in Romans 13:1–7 Paul seeks to solve a difficult problem in Rome by insisting that the Roman authorities are put there by God; and they must be obeyed and taxes must be paid to them. Not all New Testament authors would take this line. Luke (Acts 22:28) presents Paul as very proud of being a Roman citizen; but he also knew, as we shall see, that there would be a conflict between Paul's certainty that Jesus was 'Lord' and the Roman political establishment, for whom the emperor currently reigning was 'Lord'.

So those are the three strands in Paul's identity, his Jewish, Greek and Roman backgrounds. He had reservations about all of them, as we shall see, but we shall not understand him unless we grasp that he was also proud of all of them. They represent elements in his basic 'story', which for him is the story of God and of the people of God.

Paul persecuted the church

Something that we are not permitted to doubt is that Paul persecuted the emerging group that had gathered around the name of Jesus. Luke tells us so (see Acts 9:1–2, for example), as does Paul, who says of himself:

> I used to persecute the church of God
> violently, and ravaged it. (Galatians 1:13)

and:

> in my zeal [I was] persecuting the church.
> *Philippians 3:6*

In 1 Corinthians he even describes himself, in characteristically crude language, as:

> an abortion . . . not fit to be called an
> apostle, because I persecuted God's church.
> *1 Corinthians 15:8–9*

Why did he do this? He does not tell us, and neither does Luke; recently scholars have become shy of speculating about the reason for this, but we cannot help wondering. Presumably it had something to do with the story of God and of the people of God with which he had grown up. There are two obvious suggestions, neither of them provable nor without their difficulties.

The first is that this Jesus-movement (they were apparently not yet called Christians – see Acts 11:26) were claiming as Messiah the one whom Deuteronomy pronounced 'accursed'. Deuteronomy 21:23 proclaims 'cursed is the one who hangs on a tree', which is precisely what happened to Jesus, and Paul significantly quotes this in Galatians 3:13, balancing it against another line from Deuteronomy (27:26) in Galatians 3:10:

> cursed is everyone who does not remain
> with all that is written in the scroll of the
> Law so as to perform it.

The second suggestion is that it is a matter of the language that those early Jesus-people felt themselves driven to use about Jesus. Paul, like all good Jews, would recite the Shema three times a day, 'Hear, O Israel, the Lord your God is one God . . .', and the monotheism enshrined in that prayer was for him at the heart of the story of God and of God's people. It may well have seemed to him that this new movement threatened this central Jewish identity-marker. Certainly he was determined to put an end to this nonsense.

Why Paul changed

But something happened; what was it? It was undeniably costly, and got him into trouble with his co-religionists:

> five times I received the 39 [lashes] from
> the Jews. *2 Corinthians 11:24*

The maximum was 40 lashes, so they normally made sure that they did not exceed the stated number by going one lower. It was a thoroughly unpleasant sanction, even with this limitation. The price was, however, one that Paul thought was worth paying (see Philippians 3:7–8). So it was something more than just adolescent rebellion that made Paul join the Jesus-movement.

In the first place, Paul is certain that he saw Jesus. In 1 Corinthians 9:1, he asks a series of quick-fire rhetorical questions that you will at your peril answer in the negative, if you are talking to St Paul:

> Am I not free? Am I not an apostle?
> Have I not seen Jesus our Lord?

This he clearly regards as common ground between himself and the Corinthians, something that he does not have to defend; he was in no doubt that he had seen Jesus.

Secondly, and here scholars may squirm with embarrassment for they do not usually go in for language of this sort, Paul fell in love with Jesus. Listen to the 'purple passage' in which he expresses the love that transformed his life:

> Who shall separate us from the love of Christ?
> Oppression? Or being in a tight corner?
> Or persecution? Or having nothing to eat,
> or nothing to wear? Or threats?
> Or the executioner's sword?
> As Scripture says, 'For your sake,
> we are being put to death all day long;
> they think of us as sheep for the abattoir.'
> No – in all these matters we conquer,
> and more than conquer,
> through the one who loved us.
> For I am convinced that neither death,
> nor life, nor angels nor the powers,
> nor things present, nor things to come,
> nor height nor depth nor any other
> creature, will be able to separate us
> from the love of God
> which is in Christ Jesus our Lord.
>
> *(Romans 8:35–39)*

It is an extraordinary passage, with the agitated list (which we can barely follow) of the things that might intervene between us and Christ's love, and the characteristically peaceful conclusion with which he comes into harbour at the end of the passage. This love is at the heart of Paul; and it is passages of this sort that make us forgive him all the prickly bits and all his obscure passages.

Thirdly, however, if Paul had seen Jesus (and he never doubted that), and had fallen in love with him, then it meant that the Jesus-movement was after all right in what they had been saying. So at Romans 1:16 he states his new position:

> You see, I am not ashamed of the gospel –
> for it is God's power for the salvation of
> everyone who comes to faith, both Jew
> (in the first place) and Gentile.

He has accepted, then, what these Jesus-people were saying, which included the wholly unexpected message that God's story was now for non-Jews as well. This is a huge turnaround, and it may be stated in the form of five electrifying and bewildering discoveries that Paul made.

Paul's five discoveries
1. It was true about the Resurrection
The first discovery had to be that it was, after all, true, what these people had been saying about the

Resurrection. If Paul had seen Jesus (and, as we have remarked, he was in no doubt that this was the case), then Jesus, who was certainly dead, had been raised from the dead.

Paul speaks of this in several places, as you would expect. Very early in what may be his earliest letter, Paul says (as something that is non-controversial between himself and his Thessalonian audience):

> we are waiting for [God's] Son from heaven,
> whom [God] raised from the dead ...
>
> *1 Thessalonians 1:10*

The point here is that Paul is not arguing for the Resurrection – it is something on which he and the Thessalonians have already agreed.

Now this is normally the case when Paul speaks of the Resurrection. Just once, however, he does feel the need to argue for it, in 1 Corinthians 15:1–8:

> I am reminding you, brothers and sisters,
> of the gospel that I gospelled to you,
> which you accepted, in which, secondly,
> you take your stand, through which,
> thirdly, you are being saved, in what terms
> I gospelled to you, if you hold it fast –
> unless your coming to faith was pointless.
>
> For I handed down to you in the first
> place, what I also received, that Christ
> died for our sins, in accordance with the
> Scriptures, and that he was buried,

> and that he was raised on the third day,
> in accordance with the Scriptures,
> and that he was seen by Peter,
> then by the Twelve.
>
> Then he was seen by more than five
> hundred brothers and sisters at once,
> of whom the majority remain until now,
> but some have fallen asleep. Then he was
> seen by James, then by all the apostles.
> And last of all, as though to an abortion,
> he appeared also to me . . .

This is the longest passage where Paul speaks of the Resurrection; it has been provoked by the fact that some of his maverick Corinthians had been denying the truth of the Resurrection; but Paul's argument simply takes the form, not of convincing them of the truth of the Resurrection, but of reminding them what he originally preached. The basic message was what people sometimes call the 'gospel of four verbs', that Jesus 'died . . . was buried . . . was raised . . . was seen' (for elegance in English I have been driven to translate the last of Paul's four uses of the expression 'was seen' as 'appeared', but that should not be taken as implying that the apparition was anything but the real thing). So the argument is simply that without the Resurrection there is no such thing as Christianity. It is precisely at the heart of Paul's gospel.

Nor is it just an academic matter, a doctrine to be learned by heart and passed on; this is something existential. Paul longs to encounter the Resurrection, as he tells his much-loved Philippians of his desire:

> to know the power of his Resurrection,
> and the solidarity in his sufferings, being
> conformed to his death, so that somehow
> I may make it to the resurrection from
> the dead.
> *Philippians 3:10–11*

(where, incidentally, the somewhat uncertain grammar is quite characteristic of St Paul).

The same uncontested certainty about the Resurrection is to be found also in Romans, Paul's longest and most reflective letter, for example at 4:23–25 and 6:4–5.

2. Jesus is 'Lord'

The second discovery is that Jesus is to be properly addressed as 'Lord'. This is something that we take for granted, but it is worth noting that this was for Paul and those early Christians subversive from two points of view. In the first place, 'Lord' (*Kyrios/Kyrie* in Greek) is the way in which the sacred and unpronounceable name of God is represented in the manuscripts of the Greek translation of the Old Testament, which most Jews would have been using at this time. Secondly, it was a title that Roman emperors were starting to apply to themselves. So it would inevitably mean trouble on two fronts.

'Lord', however, was the way Paul had to address and speak of Jesus; in chapter three, we shall be looking at the implications of this for what he believed about Jesus. For the moment, watch him as he applies it to Jesus. So, for instance, in Romans 6:9 he declares that:

> Christ, having been raised from the dead,
> death no longer lords it over him (the verb
> 'lords' here is connected with the noun *Kyrios*).

Or consider this well-known passage from Philippians 2:9–11, which we shall look at several times during the course of this book:

> Therefore God has raised him to the
> loftiest height, and given him the free gift
> of the Name which is above every [other]
> name, in order that at the name of Jesus
> every knee should bow, of those in heaven
> and those on earth and those under the
> earth, and every tongue confess
> that Jesus Christ is LORD,
> to the glory of God the Father.

He makes the same point, later in that letter, when he speaks of:

> the surpassing greatness of [the] knowledge
> of Christ Jesus my LORD   *Philippians 3:8*

For Paul, this assertion of Jesus' lordship was a lived reality, not something to be recited in doctrine classes; and it transformed his life.

3. Jesus was indeed God's Messiah

The third discovery is the connected one, that Jesus must after all have been the Messiah that Israel had been waiting for. At first, as we shall see, this must have seemed incredible to Paul, given the manner of Jesus' dying; but given his unambiguous encounter with Jesus, it became something that he simply had to assert:

> For the Son of God, Jesus Christ, the one who was proclaimed among you through us . . ., was not 'Yes' and 'No'; on the contrary, 'Yes' happened in him; for as many as were the promises of God, [God's] 'Yes' was in him . . . *2 Corinthians 1:19–20*

Two points need to be made here. Firstly, Paul is under attack from the Corinthians, because at the end of 1 Corinthians he had said that he would be coming to them; but he never turned up, so they have charged him with fickleness. As always, he reacts sharply to criticism; and, as always, he responds by setting his answer in the context of the story of God. So here, Jesus is represented as God delivering on his promise to send a Messiah.

Secondly, the word 'Son' refers to the expected Messiah, who, like David (see Psalm 2:7, 'you are my Son'), was God's definitive answer to Israel's plight, and that is how we must understand the word in this context. Jesus is the definitive next step in the story of God and the people of God.

4. It is all grace

The fourth discovery is the all-important one for Paul, that this is all God's doing, not a matter of human achievement. The word for that in Paul is 'grace', God's unconditional free gift, something that we find very hard to imagine, or even to live with, for we always suppose that we have to *deserve* God's goodness. Paul is adamantly opposed to the idea that there is 'no such thing as a free lunch'. Listen to this ecstatic passage towards the end of Romans 8:

> We know that for those who love God, everything works together for good, for those who were called in accordance with [the divine] purpose. For those whom [God] foreknew, he also marked out beforehand as shaped in the likeness of his Son, so that his Son should be the firstborn of many brothers and sisters. And those whom he marked out beforehand, he also called; and those whom he called, he also justified, and those whom he justified he also glorified.
>
> *Romans 8:28–30*

This passage has often been read as implying predestination; don't worry about that difficult problem for the moment. The key thing here is God's free gift, irrespective of human merit. That was one of the discoveries that changed Paul's life.

5. Those who are 'in Christ' have to be different

The fifth discovery, finally, is that in consequence of this extraordinary gift of God, Jesus' followers have to be *different*. Christ, for Paul, and for those whom Paul addresses, is to be absolutely everything. Consider the following statements by him:

> For me, to live is Christ. *Philippians 1:21*

> I live now, no longer I, but Christ lives in
> me; [the life] which I live now in the flesh,
> I live by faith in the Son of God,
> who loved me and gave himself for me.
> *Galatians 2:20*

> Become imitators of me, just as I in my
> turn [have become] an imitator of Christ.
> *1 Corinthians 11:1*

These passages give a flavour of the total obsession with Jesus that governed the rest of Paul's life. If Christians have to be utterly taken over by Christ, then that entails a certain kind of behaviour.

Four consequences for Paul

These, then, were the discoveries that followed upon Paul's encounter with Jesus. They brought with them, of course, certain consequences.

1. God in Christ is the only absolute

In the first place, a good many things that Paul had hitherto held dear are now relativised. Circumcision, for example, had been one of the essential boundary-markers of the Judaism with which he grew up; but Paul came to see, perhaps in the same breath as his discovery (see no. 2 below) that he was entrusted with the mission to the Gentiles, that circumcision was after all not all that important, and that it and the Law (or 'Torah') under which he had been educated might even get in the way of Christ.

Note this strong language:

> Look – I Paul, am telling you that if you get circumcised, Christ will be of no help to you. I am testifying that anyone who is circumcised is bound to perform the entire Torah. You people who find your justification in Torah, you have been estranged from Christ.
> *Galatians 5:2–4*

Or this, a few verses later:

> I wish that those who are disturbing you might castrate themselves. *Galatians 5:12*

We mop our brow at this, and urge Paul to remember that there are ladies present, but we must not miss the point, which is that the *only* thing that matters is Christ, and not all those other things by which Paul had structured his life.

2. Non-Jews belong in God's story

Secondly, and audaciously, Paul now claims that the Gentiles belong in God's story, and that Paul himself has the task of telling them that story.

This is an important issue in Romans, probably because that letter was written to a church where there was tension between the Jewish Christians who had founded it, and the Gentile Christians who had taken it over. So in the opening salutation of that very assiduously diplomatic epistle he speaks of the:

> grace and mission that we have received
> for faithful obedience among the Gentiles.
>
> *Romans 1:5*

and speaks of his desire:

> that I might have some fruit among you
> just as [I have] also among the rest of the
> Gentiles; Greek-speakers and non-Greek-
> speakers [literally 'barbarians'], wise and
> stupid – I owe a duty to them all.
>
> *Romans 1:13–14*

Controversially, he claims that they do not need the Torah or 'Law':

> for when Gentiles who do not have Torah,
> naturally perform the things of the Torah,
> these people who do not have Torah are
> a Torah for themselves. ['a law unto
> themselves', in the King James Version]
>
> *Romans 2:14*

He is certain, however, that he has a mission to them:

> I am talking to you Gentiles. In so far as
> I am Apostle of the Gentiles, I glorify my
> ministry . . .
>
> *Romans 11:13; compare Romans 15:16*

In Galatians, where his opponents have been claiming that he has got it all wrong, Paul is sufficiently annoyed to let slip a rare piece of autobiography (so we must be for ever grateful to those who so annoyed him):

> But from those who appeared to be
> something (it is no concern of mine what
> kind of person they were; God is not a
> snob), as for me, those who appeared
> [to be something] didn't add anything.
>   No – on the contrary, they saw that
> I was entrusted with the good news

for the Uncircumcision, just as Peter was [entrusted with the good news] for the Circumcision; the One who was at work in Peter for the mission to the Circumcision was at work in me too, with regard to the Gentiles.

And when they realised the grace that had been given me, James and Kephas and John, those who appeared to be 'pillars', gave me and Barnabas the right hand of solidarity, so that we were for the Gentiles and they for the Circumcision. [They just wanted] us to remember the poor, and that was precisely what I was eager to do.

Galatians 2:6–10

In Paul's earliest letter, he makes a passing reference to the success of this work, as something on which he and the Thessalonians are agreed:

[For people tell us] of what kind of a reception we had [when we came] to you, and how you turned to God, away from the idols, in order to be slaves of the living and true God.

1 Thessalonians 1:9

They were clearly Gentiles, up there in Thessalonica, at any rate for the most part; and under Paul's guidance, they came cheerfully into the Church of Christ.

3. Paul had to write letters

The third consequence is that Paul had to write letters (and if it had not been for that, we might hardly have heard of him). He was an inveterate traveller, possibly because he was determined to get the message about Jesus all over the world before Jesus should return. However, the churches that he had founded had their problems, and the message that he had left with them had to be repeated or reinforced; and sometimes new problems would arise that Paul had to try to resolve without being able to be there in person. This is how he presents the idea at 2 Corinthians 10:10–11, where the point is the contrast and comparison between Paul's presence and the substitute presence that is a letter:

> They say, 'His letters are weighty and effective,
> but his physical presence is unimpressive,
> and his rhetoric is non-existent.' People like
> that should reflect that I am just the same
> when I am present and on business as I am
> in my correspondence, when I am absent.

Letters, of course, require writers, and we know that Paul dictated his letters, for on one occasion the secretary, Tertius, sticks his head above the parapet, to greet the Roman church (Romans 16:22: *I, Tertius, the writer of this letter, greet you in the Lord*). At other times, Paul grabs the pen and adds a message. Look at

1 Corinthians 16:21; Galatians 6:11 (where the reference to 'large letters' may suggest that he was not all that good at the technical business of writing!); Colossians 4:18; and at 2 Thessalonians 3:17 (which not all scholars agree to be by Paul) there is reference to some kind of an identifying mark by which readers or hearers can know that it is from him.

The idea of 'letter' is clearly of some importance to Paul. At 2 Corinthians 3:3, he employs the word as a metaphor, describing the Corinthians as a:

> letter, from Christ, administered by us, not written in ink but in the spirit of the Living God, not on stone tablets but on the tablets of hearts of flesh.

It may be worth reflecting that if it had not been for those letters, we should know very little about Paul; interestingly, our other evidence is largely from Acts, and if you had only that, you would not know that Paul had written any letters at all. Certainly he wrote at least some letters that we do not now possess; 1 Corinthians 5:9 refers to a prior letter to that community of Christians in Corinth, and Colossians 4:16 mentions a letter to the Laodiceans, while the instruction about the collection in the early part of 1 Corinthians 16 refers to the possibility of 'letters' of authorisation that would accompany the delivery of the collection to Jerusalem.

4. The whole of creation belongs to God

Finally, Paul's encounter with Jesus carried with it the astonishing realisation that the whole of creation, and not just the Holy Land, the Temple, and his beloved fellow Jews, belong to God, and must become fully a part of God's story. Hence his determination to cover the entire known world, telling everybody about Jesus. This is what accounts for the travel plans that he reveals in Romans 15:19–20, and 23–25, in which he sketches out an arc that runs from Jerusalem to Illyricum to Rome to Spain, about as far as someone of his time and place could conceive of journeying. It is a vast vision, this of St Paul; and all because he met Jesus, and fell in love with him.

Consequences for Paul's modern reader

What about us, today? It would not have crossed Paul's mind that you would be reading about him, or poring over his letters, more than two millennia later, in whatever place you are reading or hearing these words. However, he was certainly of the view that what had happened to him ought to have its impact on all those to whom he wrote, and indeed on all those whom he met. It would not go well with Paul if we were to keep our distance and suggest that 'I think I'll sit this one out, if you don't mind, Paul'.

What might he expect to happen to us? Firstly, I am certain, he would expect us to believe in the difficult notion of 'Resurrection', and to live as though it were true. Secondly, he would want us to follow him in falling in love with Christ. Thirdly, he would expect us to 'live in Christ'; this would include living as sinlessly as Christ himself lived, as a 'new creation' (2 Corinthians 5:17); it means living in accordance with the 'fruits of the Spirit' rather than the 'works of the flesh' (Galatians 5:18–23). It means living in community or solidarity with others (Paul's word for that is *koinonia*, a term that we shall be looking at later on). It involves respect for the leaders of the community (1 Thessalonians 5:12–13; 1 Corinthians 12:28, though we notice that the charism of 'governing' comes fairly low in his list); it means having good relations with non-Christians (1 Corinthians 5:9–10, where he makes a wry point about those who sin against the sixth commandment!); and it is a matter of praying for one another, for Christianity is not something that we can do on our own (1 Thessalonians 1:2; Romans 1:9; 15:30–32).

Above all, it is the task of Paul's readers to make the dangerous and subversive proclamation that Jesus is Lord of all the earth, and to tell this story as a narrative, not of power, but of love.

Perhaps the best way of doing this would be to make our own that proudest of all Paul's boasts, that with which he opens his longest, and arguably most influential, letter: *Paul – a slave of Jesus Christ* (Romans 1:1).

What do you think happened to Paul?
Does it make any difference to us today?

Two

What did Paul write, and how?

What did he write?

It is probably worth starting this chapter by looking at what St Paul actually wrote (or rather, as we shall see in a later chapter, dictated). Here we have to make a distinction between what he wrote (or dictated) and what was written in his name. There are 13 letters in the Pauline canon (Hebrews has sometimes been attributed to him, but it is probably best to go along with the great Scripture scholar Origen, who affirmed that 'who wrote the Letter to the Hebrews, only God knows'). The order in which you will find them in your New Testament is not, alas, the order in which they were written, but is governed by the very simple criterion of length. So Romans is the longest, 1 Corinthians the second longest, and therefore 2 Corinthians follows it. The last letter in the collection is the charming little post-card known as the letter to Philemon, which we shall be reading in chapter 10.

We must admit, as I say, that not all scholars would accept that all these letters were actually written by Paul. However, there are seven letters which all would ascribe to the Apostle: Romans, 1 and 2 Corinthians, Galatians, Philippians, 1 Thessalonians and Philemon. Then there are the 'Deutero-Paulines', which many scholars think were written by Paul's followers in the next generation, namely Colossians and Ephesians;

you will find more scholars prepared to say that Colossians is Pauline than will allow the same for Ephesians, though it must be admitted that there are scholars who think that St Paul wrote them both. Somewhere into this category comes 2 Thessalonians; the problem with that is really that it is very close to 1 Thessalonians, almost to a point where it might have been based upon it; and it is hard to find a slot in the known facts of Paul's life (based on what we have in Acts) where it would easily fit. It is also thought to be less warm and personal (even, some would say, more 'boring'!) than 1 Thessalonians.

Then there are the 'Pastoral Letters', 1 and 2 Timothy and Titus, whom very few scholars would ascribe to Paul, though some scholars do hold open the possibility of Pauline authorship. It is also worth saying that 2 Timothy, the most personal of the three letters, has more partisans than the other two as possibly Pauline. Indeed, lumping them together as the Pastorals (a title that goes back to St Thomas Aquinas) is a bit misleading, because they are rather different from each other.

What are the grounds on which scholars reach these verdicts? Sometimes, it has to be admitted, it feels as though the six that are not universally accepted are thought to be 'insufficiently Protestant'; scholars feel uncomfortable when St Paul strays in the direction of something called 'Early Catholicism', which is thought to be a bad thing. So in Colossians and Ephesians you get a more elaborate doctrine of the Church as

Body of Christ (though the idea is sketched for the first time in 1 Corinthians), while in the Pastoral Letters you get the feeling that the Church is now becoming an institution, with rules for deacons and elders and the like. In addition, there are questions about the language of these letters, for in certain respects the style is quite different from the seven that are certainly by St Paul. In this book, I shall refer to Paul and St Paul as the author of all thirteen of the letters, but not much will be made to depend on that. I encourage you to read them all with an eye open to the possibility of a different author; in the books for suggested reading you will find authors who will discuss the question of authorship. Just be aware that scholars are occasionally inclined to be more emphatic about their conclusions than their argument actually warrants.

Does it matter if Paul did not write all the letters that are found in his name in your New Testament? Probably not. Sometimes people get a bit anxious, and feel that the author may in that case be attempting to deceive, which seems awkward if the text is a religious one, and if the Scriptures are in some sense inspired by the Holy Spirit. If however you do reach the conclusion that Paul is not the author of some of the letters that exist in his name, then try thinking of it as Paul's successors saying, 'This is what Paul would be saying if he were alive today.' Certainly all six of the letters that scholars have viewed with misgivings seem entirely plausible developments of Pauline positions. Indeed many people regard Ephesians as written by someone who really understood Pauline theology. You may at this point wish to mutter to yourself, 'In that case, why could he not have written it?' But I leave that to you.

When were the letters written? Unfortunately, Paul never dated them, and we have no idea. Many scholars would argue that 1 Thessalonians was the first, although there are those who would make a case for Galatians. Which came last? If Paul wrote it, then 2 Timothy is a good candidate; many people would argue for Philippians. Romans is certainly towards the end of his career, though clearly he has yet to reach Rome at that point, so it is not quite the end. In the literature, you will find some very confident claims about the dating of the various letters, and you must make up your mind what you think about all that. There is only one solid date, and that comes from a broken inscription found at Delphi which provides a time (to within a year or so) when Gallio, whom Paul met in Corinth (Acts 18:12–17), and who was the brother of the philosopher Seneca, Nero's tutor, was proconsul of Achaea, and therefore resident in Corinth. Scholars have worked industriously and argued carefully on the dating; one would have more confidence in their conclusions if they all agreed on the date and place of writing, but I have no wish to undermine the fruits of their hard labour. Read the letters, then read what the scholars say, and make up your own mind.

The shape of letters in the ancient world

A possibly more interesting question for us, as we seek to get to know the extraordinary genius who is the subject of our investigation, is 'What did Paul do with the letter format?' A glance at what you find in your New Testament will convince you that Paul's letters are not the kind of thing that you compose in your everyday correspondence. Paul is clearly doing something different.

It is not all that different, however. For most letters in the ancient world have a basic shape; this is true whether they are the more literary ventures of Cicero or Pliny that have been handed down to us, or the discoveries in the rubbish-dump of Oxyrhynchus in the Egyptian desert, the scraps left by ordinary people. Among many other documents there are papyrus letters that have been preserved thanks to the Egyptian climate, and the fact that a canal nearby has prevented the Nile from flooding and destroying the documents. These letters all tend to have the same pattern: an opening greeting, a thanksgiving, the body of the letter, and closing greetings.

Now try applying this model to what Paul writes. There is always an opening greeting. 1 Thessalonians, for example, begins:

> Paul and Silvanus and Timothy, to the
> church [or 'assembly'] of the Thessalonians in
> God the Father and the Lord Jesus Christ:
> grace to you, and peace (1:1).

It ends with another set of greetings (5:25–28):

> Brothers and sisters, pray for us. Give
> greetings to all the brothers and sisters,
> with a holy kiss. I want you to swear
> by the Lord to have this letter read
> to all the brothers and sisters. The grace of
> Our Lord Jesus Christ be with you.

After the opening, the letter proceeds to a thanksgiving (actually two thanksgivings: see 1:2 and 2:13, and compare 2 Thessalonians 1:3 and 2:13), as do all Paul's letters, except 2 Corinthians and Galatians, where he is too cross to be bothered with giving thanks. So at Galatians 1:6, where they might have been complacently expecting Paul to thank God for all their many virtues, they hear read out in the assembly these harsh words:

> I am **astonished** that you have so quickly
> shifted your position from the one who
> called you in Christ's grace to a different
> gospel. There is no other gospel!

It is in the body of the letter that we see Paul's inventive originality. If you look at Romans, for example, you will see that 1:1–15 is the opening greeting and thanksgiving, carefully adapted to the fact that he had never been to Rome and did not know the Roman church, and indeed perhaps feared that they would not receive him very well. Then 15:14–16:23 contains the closing greetings, again rather longer than the norm, for diplomatic reasons. In between however, there is an enormous body of argument (1:16–15:13), some of it very difficult, in which Paul grapples with the question of what God has done for us in Christ, how we all need it, how both Gentiles and Jews belong in God's story, how we have every ground for confidence, how the Jews now fit into the story, and how Christians in Rome should regard each other and behave towards each other. That is what makes Romans different from other letters, such as you or I might write. I have taken Romans as an example because it is the most obvious, but if you read the others you will see the same pattern of elaborating the main body of the letter to deal with his experience.

What was it that made Paul elaborate the letter form in this way? It was simply the very new thing that had happened to him in his encounter with Jesus. The letter form was an obvious way of keeping contact with groups of Christians around the Mediterranean, but it needed adaptation if it were to cope with the fact that Paul had met Jesus and that therefore God had raised Jesus from the dead. In fact, Mark found himself forced to do something similar, taking the basic literary form of a 'biography', and adapting it to what he thought God had done in Jesus. You will not understand the New Testament unless you grasp that all its authors were under pressure to do justice in their writing to a very new and unexpected phenomenon.

And you might like to consider whether the other writers of letters in the New Testament wrote in that way because Paul had done it first.

Why do people write letters?

People have a variety of reasons for writing letters, even if dinosaurs like me mutter sourly that 'the e-mail has put an end to the art of letter-writing'. The basic reason for writing a letter, when the letter form works properly, is that it is a substitute for personal presence. You cannot be there, and so a letter is the next best thing. Thus Paul clearly wishes that he could be present to the churches that he has founded, and occasionally this desire becomes very pressing. So at 1 Corinthians 5:3, when dealing with the problem of incest (to which we shall be returning in subsequent chapters), we hear him say:

> For I, although absent in body, am present
> in spirit; and I have already reached my
> verdict, as though I were present . . .

and the same yearning to be present is detectable in 1 Thessalonians 3:9–10:

> before our God, night and day, imploring,
> so as to see your face, and to make good
> what is lacking in your faith.

Characteristically in both of these instances, Paul is exercising his authority, and we may be safe in assuming that this was what he did when he was present.

One other thing is worth saying on this topic. Most of the time when we write letters, it is because we care about the person addressed; and that is certainly the case with Paul, even though he often loses his temper with his not very expert Christians. He was unmistakably fond of them. If you have a moment, read the two letters that survive of Paul's Corinthian correspondence, and count the number of times that he refers to his love for them, even though he has to tell them off, sometimes very sharply indeed.

Why did Paul write?

For the remainder of this chapter, I should like to go through 1 Thessalonians, which, as I say, may well be his earliest surviving letter, to see if we can work out what he thinks he is doing, based on what he actually does. Keep a copy of the letter somewhere near to hand, so that you can check the text against what I say.

1. To continue the experience

At 1:3–5 he shares with the Thessalonians the memory of what it was like, that time when he first came to them:

> recalling your work of faith and labour of
> love and your perseverance in hope in our

> Lord Jesus Christ before our God and
> Father, knowing, brothers and sisters,
> whom God loves, how God chose you, that
> our gospel when it reached you was not just
> a matter of formulae, but a matter of
> power and of the Holy Spirit.

Notice how the vein of reminiscence continues to the end of the chapter. He recalls not just what it was like when he was up there with them in Thessalonica, but also how it has been reported back to him since, and the effect that their response had on others (1:6–10). Then, in chapter two, he goes back to the impact that it had on him, partly by way of contrast to what had happened in Philippi (2:2) but he also reminds them of the warmth of their reception of him.

2. To reinforce the message

Next Paul moves, almost imperceptibly, from the 'do you remember . . .' style that people adopt at alumni reunions, to reminding them of the message he taught. He gives thanks (again):

> to God, that when you accepted
> the word you heard from us, as of God,
> you accepted it, not as a word of human
> beings, but as it truly is, a word from God,
> who is at work among you who believe.
>
> *1 Thessalonians 2:13*

That will turn them to thinking back on what he actually said, before he restores them to their comfort zone with some more reminiscence (2:14–20). Note the affection that pours out of every sentence; and notice, too, how Paul insists on the experience that they shared together. He never writes out of empty piety, as religious people can all too easily do; Paul always inhabits the real world, with all its harshness.

3. As a substitute for personal presence
We have mentioned this before, but it is important not to miss the affection that bubbles out as Paul speaks of his desire to be with the Thessalonians:

> As for us, brothers and sisters, we were
> orphaned of you just for a while, away
> from you in person, but never in our hearts;
> but we were even more eager to see your
> faces, with great longing (2:17).

And he continues in the same vein:

> So when we could no longer bear it,
> we decided to stay alone in Athens;
> we sent Timothy, our fellow Christian and
> fellow-worker of God in the gospel of Christ,
> to give you solidity, and to comfort you
> in your faith.

There is real love here, and we shall not understand Paul unless we grasp the towering humanity of his immense heart.

4. Because the moment requires an intervention
Sex

Preachers have from time to time felt obliged to speak of matters of sexual morality, to a point where the Church is sometimes accused of being interested only in what people do in their bedrooms. But Paul, unlike most of his converts, was brought up in the strict sexual morality of Judaism (as we shall see in chapter 12), and he knew that sex is too important to be treated carelessly. So he has to remind the Thessalonians, who had not been Jews (1:9) when they were converted, about appropriate sexual behaviour:

> This is God's will, your sanctification, to keep away from fornication *(for Paul, this is a blanket-term covering all kinds of sexual misbehaviour)*, for each of you to know how to keep his own vessel in holiness and honour *(we shall not explore the possible meanings of the term 'vessel' here; let the reader's imagination supply the lack)*, not with passionate lust, like the Gentiles who do not know God, not to go over the top and desire one's brother or sister in that matter ... for God did not call us to impurity, but to holiness (4:3–7).

Simply notice here, what we shall see again, the importance that Paul attaches to sex, because of the loving presence of God.

Loving the brothers and sisters

But it is not all about sex; and one element of discipleship to which Paul always gave priority is that of *philadelphia*, or loving the brothers and sisters. Here Paul claims that he is simply reinforcing their existing 'good practice', although we may wonder if he is not protesting too much:

> You have no need for us to write to you about *philadelphia;* for you have been God-taught to love one another. For you do that to all the saints *('saints' is Paul's word, not for dead disciples, but for those who are still living, including all the readers of this text)* in all of your part of Greece.
>
> And we are encouraging you, brothers and sisters, to abound all the more in this philadelphia; and to aspire to live quietly, and to do your own thing, and to work with your own hands, just as we told you, so that you may have a good relationship with outsiders, and have no need of anything.
>
> *1 Thessalonians 4:9–12*

Resurrection

At the heart of Paul's gospel is the message of the Resurrection. Not only does he insist on the claim that God raised Jesus from the dead; he also asserts that this has implications for those who are followers of Jesus. In every generation, however, this strikes people as 'news too good to be true', and so Paul has to reinforce the message that he has already given them (and we shall do well to reflect upon it ourselves). Probably they had started to wonder about those in their community who had died, whether they had missed what Jesus came to bring. So he reassures them:

> We don't want you to be ignorant, brothers and sisters, about those who have fallen asleep; we don't want you to grieve as other people do, those who have no hope. For if we believe that Jesus died and rose again, so also God, through Jesus, will bring along with him those who have fallen asleep.
>
> *1 Thessalonians 4:13–14*

Then in the following verses (4:15–5:11) he uses language taken from Jewish texts that imagine what it will be like when God finally intervenes, to give the Thessalonian Christians a feel of what they might expect. We are not intended to read it all literally, though; the point of it is to console the Thessalonians with the certainty that death is not the end, thanks to what God has done in Christ. Literal readings of this passage have led to the unhealthy doctrine of the 'rapture', the view that people just disappear, for example in the course of aeroplane journeys, 'snatched up' with Christ. That is not what Paul is speaking about, but the unfailing fidelity of God. The main point in the opening verses of chapter 5 is that you simply do not know, and have no way of telling, when God will intervene. All that we know is that God in Christ is not going to let us down.

Authority in the congregation

There is one last issue that Paul considers before he goes into his concluding remarks and greetings (5:16–28), and that is the matter of authority. Paul's gift was to start Christian groups; but he knew perfectly well that, human nature being what it is, they would not just go on functioning as Christian groups unless they had some identifiable structure (and I hope that I shall not be charged here with propagating 'early Catholicism'!). So he reminds them of the appropriate response to those whom he has left in charge:

> We are asking you, brothers and sisters, to
> recognise those who labour among you,
> and who are in charge of you in the Lord,
> and who admonish you. [We want you] to
> regard them, beyond all measure, with love,
> because of the work that they do. Be at
> peace among yourselves . . .
>
> *1 Thessalonians 5:12–13*

This is quite an important passage in this first of Paul's letters; already he knows the need for a degree of what nowadays we call by that ugly word 'institutionalisation'. It is simply not the case that those who believe in Jesus automatically get things right, and need no sort of authority among them.

What do the letters conceal?

Letters are (normally) a very personal literary form, a way of pouring ourselves out on paper. But we need to be careful here: letters do not always give us everything that we should like to know. This is for two reasons, both of which apply to all letters, including those written by Paul.

The first reason is that when, as is the case with the Pauline letters, we do not have the letters to which the author is responding, or which he elicited from his correspondents, we have only one half of the debate. Very often (and we shall see this in particular when we look at the letters that he wrote to Corinth) we simply do not know what is going on, whereas those who heard his letters read out to them knew perfectly well. As many scholars have helpfully suggested, it is like listening to just one side of a telephone conversation, which can be a very frustrating experience.

The second reason is that inevitably when we are writing letters we have a particular aim in mind, or, sometimes, several aims. Those aims, however, will not always correspond with what we as modern readers are looking for. Paul will have had his private agenda in all that he wrote, and was not trying to answer the many questions that we should still like to be putting to him. Such questions might include the following:

> When did you write this letter, Paul?
> What was going on in the place to which
>   you were writing?

Why did you emphasise the points that you
   did, and not others?
Did you really write all the letters that are
   ascribed to you?
Were all the letters written as they have
   come down to us?

What do the letters reveal?

One of the difficulties about the way most of us receive Paul's letters is that they are heard read out in church. In a sense, that is not too bad, because that is how Paul originally envisaged them; they were not intended for private reading and meditation, because most of Paul's Christians will not have been able to read. So they will have been performed, by someone with the gift for proclaiming them; and they will have been received by the group, not by individuals.

When we receive them, however, it is for the most part in short bursts, taken out of context, and because it is the inspired word of God, and because we are going to say 'Thanks be to God' at the end of it, we tend to suppose that there can be nothing in it for us. That is a dreadful (though understandable) mistake. If you get nothing else from this book, I'd like you to put it down with a strong sense that Paul's letters reveal a flesh-and-blood person, who can be angry and affectionate by turns, who is in love with Jesus, and desperate for the world to know about his beloved, and that Christians should live out the gospel as it should be lived. Paul is no plaster saint, but a real person, prickly and defensive as well as a great lover. As you read what he writes, try to come to grips with the real human being who dictated these extraordinary texts.

Which letters do you think Paul wrote?
Does it matter if he did not write all the letters that are attributed to him?
Why did he write 1 Thessalonians?

Three
Did Paul think that Jesus was God?

The answer is obvious

You might wonder why the question about Paul's view of Jesus' divine status is even raised; isn't the answer perfectly obvious? I have often found myself exhorting young people to some improbable virtue, and urging them on by way of the observation that this is how Jesus operated. And they often reply, 'It was all very well for him – he was God, wasn't he?', as though that ended the matter.

It is not quite as simple as that, however. For the first heresy that the Church had to contend with is one into which we can all too easily drift today; it was called 'Docetism', and it consisted basically in the view that Jesus only *seemed* to be human, and was really God-in-disguise. That is what the young people are saying when they resist my appeal to Jesus' example; and Paul would have had no time at all for this notion.

There is a further point here, that Paul, like all the early Christians, was a good Jew, and, then as now, good Jews recited the Shema three times a day, with its key assertion, 'Hear, O Israel; the Lord your God is *one* God'. It is possible that this is the source of Paul's first reaction to the Christian movement; he may have decided that it had to be eliminated, because it was using of Jesus language that should be reserved for God. Undoubtedly Paul's thought went through something of a revolution; but it is important to say at the outset of this chapter (which will undoubtedly be the hardest in this book, so make sure that you are feeling fresh when you attempt it) that Paul never abandoned this basic Jewish insight. Paul was and remained a monotheist, for whom there is and can be, only one God. It is true that as a Jew of his time and place he was almost certainly familiar with the possibility of other ways of talking of God's action in the world; for example, his fellow Jews might speak of 'God's Spirit' at work in the world, or of the 'Wisdom of God', and at times the way they spoke of these two might have made them sound like 'hypostatisations', or alternative personifications of God. But Paul was never a pagan, so he would never lapse into the pagan error of failing to see that human beings are not God, but are made in God's image and likeness (see Genesis 1:27); he was at no point in danger of idolatry.

Paul redefines monotheism

Yet even though Paul never ceased to be a monotheist, it is important to recognise the extraordinary revolution in thinking that he either embraced or originated (embraced if he was simply following what other fellow Christians said about Jesus, originated if it was he who started this way of talking). For Paul, without ever abandoning the monotheism in which he had grown up, nevertheless redefined it, in order to do justice to the Christian experience of Jesus and of that mysterious reality to which they gave the name of 'Spirit'.

We can see Paul at work on this matter of preserving his ancestral monotheism while at the same time doing justice to the experience of those first Christians, as we look at four important texts. And actually it is perhaps not correct to speak of Paul as 'at work', because in all these texts, the position he adopts is assumed, and he feels no need to argue for it; so presumably his audience in Rome, Philippi, Corinth and Colossae will have agreed with the way he reads the Scriptures.

1. Romans 10:5–13

> For Moses writes of the justification that comes from Law: 'The person who does them will live by them.' But this is how the justification that comes from faith speaks: 'Don't say in your heart, "Who will go up to heaven?" *(i.e. to bring Christ down)*, or "Who will go down into the abyss?" *(i.e. to bring Christ up from the dead)*.
>
> What does it say? 'The word is near to you, in your mouth and in your heart.' *(i.e. the word of faith that we proclaim)*. Because if you confess with your mouth that Jesus is Lord, and believe in your heart that God raised him from the dead, you will be saved.
>
> For the believing takes place in the heart – and that leads to justification, while the

> confessing takes place in the mouth – and that leads to salvation. For Scripture says, 'Nobody who believes in him will be put to shame.' For there is no distinction between Jew and Gentile, for the same one is Lord of all, dispensing his wealth to all those who call upon him, for 'Everyone who calls on the name of the Lord will be saved.'

It is important to remember the context. Paul has finished the difficult argument supporting his view that what God has done in Christ means that the good news goes out to the entire human race – it is not just Jews, but also Gentiles, who are to be welcomed into the group of Jesus' disciples. Now (in chapters 9–11) he is working out the further implications of this: what does this mean for Paul's fellow Jews, whom he longs to see 'in Christ'? At the heart of what Paul is saying is the distinction between 'justification that comes from Law', and 'justification that comes from faith'. For Paul, the latter has now replaced the former; but more important than that, it has done so in Jesus. So Paul quotes from Deuteronomy, chapters 9 and 30; and the point he is making is that God in Christ has bridged the hitherto uncrossable gap between Creator and creation. So it is God who has brought us the Messiah (Christ); and it is God who has raised him from the dead. So far so good; but the next step is the tricky one. The next step is to argue that Jesus is 'Lord'; and here Paul does not mean anything less than what the Old Testament means by God. At no point in the above verses does Paul feel the need to argue his point; he simply assumes that the Romans already agree with the position he has taken up here, and that he can use this as a basis for his argument that the Jews belong within God's plan. It is breathtaking, this position that Paul outlines, an astonishingly rich understanding of God.

2. Philippians 2:1–11

This is a famous passage; but we need to hear it attentively. Many scholars argue that it is earlier than Paul, and that he is quoting to the Philippians a 'hymn' that is already familiar to them. Once again, notice that he does not argue for it; here he is using it in order to stop the Philippians quarrelling (see 2:1–5 and 4:2):

> If there is any encouragement in Christ,
> if there is any consolation in love, if there
> is any solidarity in the Spirit, if there is any
> compassion or mercy, fill up my joy, and
> have the same mindset, the same love, a
> unity of spirit, having a single mindset,
> nothing by way of selfishness or empty
> conceit. No – in humility [I want you to]
> think of each other as superior to yourselves,
> each of you looking, not to your own
> interests, but to the interests of others.
>
> [I want you to] have that mindset which
> was also in Christ Jesus, who being in the

> form of God, did not think that equality
> with God was a snatching-matter. No –
> he emptied himself, taking on the form
> of a slave (!), turning up in the likeness
> of a human being. And being found
> in appearance as a human being, he humbled
> himself, being obedient to the point of
> death (even death on the cross!).
>
> Because of that, God raised him up to
> the very highest, and gave him the free gift
> of the name that is above every name,
> so that at the name of Jesus, every knee
> should bow, of those in heaven, and those
> on earth, and those under the earth,
> and every tongue confess that Jesus Christ
> is Lord, to the glory of God the Father.

One thing that you should notice about this passage is that it actually wobbles a bit between language that suggests that Jesus is indeed God, and language that suggests an inferior status. For example, it starts with Jesus 'in the form of God', but then mentions that, 'equality was not a snatching-matter'. Then it continues by emphasising what we should call the divinity of Jesus, 'emptied himself, taking on the form of a slave, turning up in the likeness of a human being'. On the other hand, he is 'obedient', presumably to God; and it is God who gives him the name above all other names. Then again, Jesus is raised up 'to the very highest', he is 'Lord', and he has the 'name which is above every other name', all of which suggests a very lofty status indeed. What is going on here? I suggest that Paul, or his predecessor, is using language that grasps at the (ultimately ungraspable) reality of Jesus, that he is both human and divine, trying to hold both realities together. And if this composition is indeed earlier than Paul, we must assume that Paul agrees with what it is saying; otherwise, he would not quote it in this pastoral context of persuading the Philippians not to quarrel any more.

There is a further point here. The language is unmistakably Jewish, and there is a clear allusion to Isaiah 45:23 in *every knee should bow . . . every tongue confess.* Significantly, that part of Second Isaiah is a passage given over to preserving Israel's monotheism against those in Babylon who would worship idols. So we have an affirmation of Jesus' divinity precisely where Paul's hearers would have detected his certainty that there is indeed only one God. There is only one God, but the understanding of God is expanded and enriched to include the story of Jesus. We are here eavesdropping on some explosively new thinking about God.

3. 1 Corinthians 8:4–6

We have already mentioned the Shema, 'Hear, O Israel; the Lord your God is one God'. Now comes a passage in which Paul actually quotes it. The context is Paul's attempt to resolve a question that the Corinthians have raised about whether or not it is permissible to eat food that has been sacrificed to idols. The point here is that to buy in the market food that has been sacrificed in one of the Corinthian temples is a cheap way of getting hold of necessary protein in the ancient world. It looks as though some people in Corinth were arguing that 'we all know' that there is no such thing as other gods, and therefore it does not matter whether or not we eat such meat; we know what we are doing, and they are not real gods. Paul is quite sympathetic to that point of view (see 8:4–5), although in the end he is going to argue, in verses 7–13 of chapter 8, that for the sake of fellow Christians who are not quite so adaptable, it may be better to avoid what could turn out to be an occasion for scandal.

Once again, therefore, the context is a pastoral one, and, once again, there is an echo of an Old Testament passage that asserts Israel's monotheism. Listen to what Paul writes here, and hear his quotation of the Shema.

> As for the eating of food offered to idols, we know that there is no such thing as an idol in the universe, and there is no god except the one God. For even if there are many so-called 'gods' in heaven and on earth, so that there are many 'gods' and many 'lords', nevertheless, we have one God (the Father), from whom everything comes, and we are for him, and one Lord (Jesus Christ), through whom everything comes and we are through him.

Paul quite deliberately quotes that all-important mantra of monotheism, but expands it to include Jesus as 'Lord' within the Jewish story of God. As in the previous two passages, there is no indication whatever that Paul thinks that he will have to argue for it. What he is arguing for is a solution to the ticklish question, about food offered to idols, that has presented itself to the Corinthian Christians. Again, we see here signs of audacious and creative theological thinking, whether by Paul himself or someone else, under the pressure of the encounter with the Risen Jesus.

4. Colossians 1:15–20

Our final passage is from Colossians; and, as we have already indicated, there are scholars who do not think that this is from St Paul's pen, but we are probably safe to use it as an indicator of what Paul might think about Jesus, the more so as in the context the author is trying to get the Colossians to walk worthily of the Lord,

> so as to be utterly pleasing in all good works
> (Colossians 1:10),

in the context of a heretical movement, whose contours we can no longer confidently reconstruct.

One other thing to say about this passage is that the sentence in which it is found starts all the way back at verse 9, and is one of the longest sentences in the entire New Testament.

It is probably worth going back to the beginning of the sentence, at verse 9:

> Because of this, we too, from the day when we heard [about it] do not cease from giving thanks, praying for you, and asking that you may be filled with the knowledge of [God's] will, in all wisdom and spiritual understanding, to walk worthily of the Lord, to please him in every way, in every good work, bearing fruit and growing in the knowledge of God, empowered in all power, according to the might of his glory, for all endurance and patience, with joy, giving thanks to the Father who makes you fitted for the portion of the lot of the holy ones in light, who delivered you from the power of darkness, and transferred you into the kingdom of the Son of his love, in whom we have redemption, the forgiveness of sins, who is the likeness of the unseen God, the first-born of all creation, because everything was created in him, in heaven and on earth, things seen and things unseen, whether thrones or lordships or rulers or authorities, all were created through him and towards him, and he is before everything, and everything holds together in him, and he is the head of the body, the church, he is the beginning,

> the first-born from the dead, that he
> himself might become Number One in
> everything, because in him the whole
> Fullness was pleased to dwell, and through
> him to reconcile everything to him, making
> peace by the blood of his cross, whether
> things on earth or things in heaven.

Whenever this was written, and whoever is the author, we clearly have to do here with a very lofty doctrine of who Jesus is. He is called 'Son', which need mean no more than 'Messiah' (although that is already quite a high status). At a higher level, Jesus is the 'likeness of the unseen God' (as a former teacher of mine used to say, 'if you want to know what God is like, look at Jesus'); at the same time, however, he is first-born of all creation, which might imply that Jesus is created, and might also carry a reference to Jesus' Resurrection.

If however *everything was created in him*, then it seems that he is not, after all, created. Certainly, this text places Jesus way above ordinary secular or spiritual powers (*thrones . . . lordships . . . rulers . . . authorities*), which were, in a remarkable expression, *created through him and towards him*. So Jesus is *before everything*, and is the *beginning*; here some scholars think that Paul may be reflecting on the opening words of the Bible, 'in the beginning God created the heavens and the earth', and reflecting on the different possible meanings of the Hebrew word for 'beginning', which might include 'head' and 'first-born' and 'Number One'. Most striking of all is the line that *the whole Fullness* dwelt in him. That can only mean the Deity, and it is a very high claim indeed, on the part of this unashamed monotheist.

Lastly, we need to notice that who Jesus was is intimately connected with what Jesus does, in the mind of Paul, and we shall be looking at that in the next chapter. For the moment, simply notice that 'what Jesus does' includes notions like 'delivered', 'redemption', 'forgiveness', 'reconcile', 'making peace', and most enigmatic of all a reference to the 'blood of his cross'.

The big question: was Jesus God?

You may think that what we have said so far answers the question; if Paul can use this kind of language about Jesus, then can he say anything less than that Jesus was indeed divine? That is pressing things too hard, however. Remember that Paul is a good Jew, and good Jews are wired not to go around the place saying that human beings are God. That is what pagans do; and we are not pagans. None of the verses that we have looked at so far, you will observe, actually *says* that Jesus is God. Indeed, we saw when looking at that startling passage, 1 Corinthians 8:6, that Paul separates the two parts of the Shema, so that 'God' refers to the Father, and 'Lord' to Jesus.

There are however three possible passages where Paul has sometimes been taken as referring to Jesus as

God. We shall take them in reverse order, both as to probable date, and as to plausibility of finding a reference here to Jesus as God.

The first text is Titus 2:11–13:

> For the grace of the saving God
> has appeared to all human beings, disciplining
> us to deny impiety and worldly passions,
> so as to live in a sober and just and pious
> manner in the present age, waiting
> for the happy hope and the appearance
> of the glory of our great God and Saviour,
> Jesus Christ.

Does this carry a claim that Jesus is the 'great God and Saviour'? Probably not, we should have to say, in the light of Paul's usage elsewhere. I ask you simply to notice that it is one possible reading of the text. Another possible reading would be to take 'Jesus Christ' as 'Saviour'; and a third is to understand it as saying that 'Jesus Christ is the *glory* of our great God and Saviour'. The third of these seems the more likely to me; I simply want you to notice the various possibilities, and to reflect that if Paul exercises a properly Jewish caution about directly ascribing divinity to Jesus in other places, and if it is not clear that this is what he intends here, then we too may be appropriately cautious. We do not have to suppose that Paul must have reached the position eventually adopted by the Council of Chalcedon (the fourth Ecumenical Council, which in the year 451 finally decided how Christians should talk about the humanity and divinity of Christ).

The second text is 2 Thessalonians 1:12:

> ... that the name of our Lord Jesus
> may be glorified in you, and you in him,
> according to the grace of our God and Lord,
> Jesus Christ
> **or**: according to the grace of our God and
> of the Lord Jesus Christ.

This text can be translated in either of the above-mentioned ways. Once again, it is probably best to stick with Paul's normal usage, and see *according to the grace* as governing two individuals, namely God and Jesus Christ; and we might reflect that Paul very often mentions Jesus and the Father in a single sentence, but clearly as two different persons, for example in 1 Corinthians 1:3, 'grace to you and peace from God our Father and from the Lord Jesus Christ' (compare Romans 1:7 and many other places that you can find for yourself).

Our final text, and the one that might give us most pause, is Romans 9:5.

You have to remember that in Paul's original text there will have been no punctuation; the helpful-looking punctuation marks in your texts of the New Testament are, I regret to inform you, no better than guesses on the part of editors and translators. With that in mind, now read what the text says. At the beginning of

Romans 9–11, there is a long passage of argument where Paul wrestles with the question of how his fellow Jews fit into God's plan. He first lists their advantages:

> Israelites, theirs is the adoption-as-sons, and the glory, and the covenants and the Law-giving, and the cult and the promises; theirs are the ancestors (Romans 9:4).

Then he continues with this half-line:

> ... and from them comes Christ (or: the Messiah) according to the flesh, the one who is God above all, blessed for ever, Amen.

Read it that way, and it seems unambiguously a claim that Jesus is God. That is not the only way of reading it, however (remember that there is no punctuation in the original), and it might have been:

> ... and from them comes the Messiah according to the flesh. May God who is above all be blessed for ever. Amen.

How are we to decide? Well you must make up your own mind, based on how you read St Paul. But in so very Jewish a passage, it seems highly unlikely that Paul would bless the Messiah as God, quite apart from the point that we have already made, that Paul splits up the Shema prayer, so that 'the Father' is everywhere else reserved for God, and 'the Lord' always refers to Jesus in the Pauline writings. And it may be worth pointing out that there is a similar blessing of God in Romans 11:33–36, and that Paul may be sandwiching the argument of this very dense section between the two blessings of God. It is not that Paul does not think that Jesus is divine; it is more that he does not say so – and that silence is something that we should respect. At the heart of Paul's experience of Jesus, and that which turned his life quite upside down, is the insight that 'God raised Jesus from the dead' (Romans 10:9, for example), and it is hard to see how Paul can write that if in some simple sense he thought that Jesus and God were identical.

This is a difficult area in which to wander, and it is important not to be too hasty in reaching a conclusion: how *do* you talk sensibly about Jesus and his relationship to God, never mind reconstructing the views of the long-dead Paul? What is clear is the order in which it happens, in Paul's mind. First, his meeting with Jesus starts a lifelong devotion to him; then he recognises what Jesus has done for us (which we shall be looking at in the next chapter). Only after that does the question arise: in that case, who was Jesus? And the maddening thing is that Paul does not really answer that question, or rather, he assumes that he and his correspondents agree on it, since the Christological passages that we have been looking at come in all kinds of different contexts. At no point does he have to sit down and convince them about who Jesus is.

There is however just one thing that we should notice, before we move on, and that is that what Paul now believes about God is richer than anything that he could have known as a youngster being trained up within Judaism. For from now on, Paul has to include in the age-old Israelite story of the one God, not merely the one he calls 'Father', but also 'Jesus Messiah' and the 'Holy Spirit'. Look how it works out in this passage (1 Corinthians 12:4–6). Remember as you do so that at this point in the letter Paul is trying to work on the pastoral problem of the divisions within the Corinthian church based on the very different spiritual gifts that they had within the body. So he writes:

> There are divisions of gifts – but the same
> Spirit. And there are divisions of ministries –
> but the same Lord. And there are divisions
> of activities – but the same God, who
> enacts all in all.

This leads him into a breathtaking solution to the problem of divisions in Corinth; for in the next few verses he starts to outline his vision of the Church as body; and the theological point that he is making is that he wants to find in the Corinthian Body of Christ the same unity in diversity as he finds in the story of God, as that story has to be retold after his encounter with the Risen Jesus. We can feel ourselves here watching a key moment of creative thinking about God, on the part of one who stands on the edge of a very important moment in the history of theology.

NOT THAT MAN!

How do you think Jesus fits into the story of God?
Do you agree with what Paul thinks of Jesus?
Did Paul think that Jesus was God?

Four
What did Jesus do for us?

He died for our sins

Once again, you may feel that the answer is obvious. Paul expresses in 1 Corinthians 15:3, that 'he died for our sins'. Certainly, generations of Christians have recited this phrase and found help in it. The difficulty comes when you try to examine what it might mean. However, it is a good starting point. It looks as though the origin of Paul's difficulty with the Jesus-movement may have been the fact that Jesus died precisely on the cross; and perhaps he may in addition have had problems with Jesus' attitude to the Law. When he is writing his very cross letter to the Christians in Galatia, in chapter 3, just as he is about to start the difficult argument about Abraham, he quotes Deuteronomy twice. First, he cites 27:26, 'Cursed is anybody who does not abide by the things written in the scroll of the Law, to perform them.' Then he quotes 21:23, 'Cursed is anybody who hangs on the tree.' In between those two, however, he quotes the line from Habakkuk which became so important to him, here and in Romans, 'The just person shall live as a result of faith.' This neatly captures the revolution that had taken place in Paul's thought. For the one who had held such a casual attitude to Law, and who had (deservedly therefore) been crucified, was alive, and Paul had seen him. That meant that it was true about the Resurrection;

and that in turn meant that the Jesus-movement was correct in identifying Jesus as God's Messiah. That meant that a) Law did not have the importance that Paul had earlier supposed and b) that something else, or, rather, someone else, had taken its place. And to that someone else, the appropriate response was faith, leading to life in God (and in Christ).

Now, if Jesus was indeed the Messiah, then the Cross had to be taken seriously; instead of being a disgusting punishment, this criminal's death was (somehow or other) part of God's plan. So when Paul is pushing the argument about Abraham a bit further, in Romans, he quotes another favourite Old Testament line, from Genesis 15:6, 'It was reckoned to him as righteousness.' The point here for Paul is that Abraham was given God's righteousness, not because he was circumcised or Law-observant (Abraham is not circumcised until Genesis 17:23–27; and the Law has not been given yet), but because he believed in God. After that citation, Paul continues (Romans 4:23–25):

> It was not written on his account alone,
> that 'it was reckoned to him'. No – it was also
> on account of us, us who are about to have
> it reckoned, us who believe in the One who
> raised Jesus from the dead, [Jesus] who was
> handed over because of our sins, and raised
> because of our justification.

Here Paul is engaged in some quite dense theological thinking. The progress of his thought seems to be as follows:

- Jesus was raised from the dead by God. Therefore
- Jesus was God's Messiah.
- So God had vindicated Jesus, including his casual attitude to Law.
- So, somehow, Jesus' death was important,
- and it had to do with 'our sins' [we might talk about 'getting us out of the mess we have made'].
- Much more important, however, was the Resurrection, which is God's verdict ('justification') on the whole affair.

If this is right, then what counts is not the death of Jesus, but his Resurrection. Now of course there is no Resurrection without a death; and the Cross remains a huge theological problem for Christians (for both Paul and ourselves). Paul's emphasis, however, remains, as ours must, on the victory that God won in Jesus.

And there is a further problem. If God is in charge, and if Jesus' death was part of the plan, are we dealing with a God who demanded blood to pacify his wrath with regard to human sinfulness? Most people would be uncomfortable with this view of the God of love, even though they might admit that the fact of human sinfulness has to be dealt with, somehow or other. Let us examine whether Paul held that view.

Jesus expiated our sins

There is a place in Romans where Paul might be read as thinking in this way. He writes:

> As it is, God's righteousness has shone
> forth, apart from Law, authenticated by the
> Law and by the Prophets, the righteousness
> of God through faith in Jesus Christ
> [**or**: through the faith of Jesus Christ],
> [reaching out] to **all** those who believe
> (for there is no distinction).
>
> For all sinned and fell short of the glory
> of God, being justified as a free gift by his
> unconditional love [**or**: grace] through the
> redemption [literally: buying-back] which
> was in Christ Jesus, whom God publicly
> displayed as a *hilasterion* through faith,
> by means of his blood, to reveal his [God's,
> presumably] justification on account of
> the forgiveness of the sins that have gone
> before, in God's forbearance, to reveal his
> justification at the present time, so that
> God is just, and justifies those who live out
> of faith in Jesus [**or**: Jesus' faith].
>
> *Romans 3:21–26*

This is an important passage, and, once again, quite a dense one. Unhappily, it is not absolutely plain sailing to translate. Perhaps the most awkward term is the one that I have left in Greek, *hilasterion*. In the Greek Old Testament, this word normally translates as the 'mercy-seat', and it has sacrificial connotations, as the use of the word 'blood' suggests that it may have here. We bristle uncomfortably at this, as though Jesus were a piece of raw meat thrown to an angry God to calm the divine anger that our sinfulness has justly provoked. The word 'propitiate', which is sometimes used in this context, carries the uncomfortable hint of precisely that tyrannous deity. 'Atonement', or reconciliation, is an easier notion for us to manage.

Nevertheless, it is clear that for Paul the death of Jesus was important in some way, and he is here linking it to what the High Priest does in the Holy of Holies on the Day of Atonement. In a well-known, and in some ways alarming, comment on what God did in Jesus, Paul writes:

> The one who did not know sin,
> [God] made into sin [**or**: 'a sin-offering']
> on our behalf, so that we might become
> God's justification in him.
>
> *2 Corinthians 5:21*

This is a remarkably shocking thing for Paul to say (and compare Galatians 3:13 for shock-value: *Christ bought us back from the curse of the law, becoming a curse for our sake*). Somehow or other, the death of Jesus is God's way of dealing with the catastrophe that sin had wreaked upon the human race. We are not to regard Jesus as a 'substitute', who takes the punishment that we deserve; we are all going to die, after all. Perhaps we should think of Jesus as our 'representative'. Simply notice that how it works is not easy for us to grasp, and it might be that Paul would have scratched his head if we had asked him about it. Perhaps, though, we can say the following:

- God has done something massive for us in Christ.
- That 'something massive' has to do with the fact that, from our angle, we are sinners and unable to do anything about it.
- From the other angle, it has to do with Jesus' death.
- It is part of the 'story of God' (the Law and the Prophets).
- It is God's 'free gift' ('grace').
- It means that the story is now open, not merely to Jews, but also to non-Jews.
- Paul can only reach for the meaning of what he is trying to say in metaphors like righteousness/justification, 'grace', 'redemption', and *hilasterion*.

Christ reverses what Adam did

One way that Paul has of expressing what Jesus did, is to speak of the plight in which humanity finds itself as 'what Adam brought about', so that Adam stands for the whole of humanity. There are two passages where Paul speaks of this.

The first comes when Paul is trying to persuade the Corinthians of the centrality of the Resurrection (1 Corinthians 15:20–22):

As it is, Christ has been raised from the
dead, the first fruits of those who have
fallen asleep. For since Death came through
a human being, it was also through a human
being that Resurrection from the dead
came. You see, as in Adam all humans die,
so in Christ all humans will be made alive.

Here, the notion is that what God has done in Jesus puts human beings into a different place. Death is the consequence of human disobedience; Resurrection is the consequence of Jesus' obedience. Then, later in the same chapter (15:42–49), Paul looks at the question of how (in what form, perhaps) the dead are raised:

So it is with the Resurrection from the
dead. It is sown in corruption, but raised in
incorruptibility; it is sown in dishonour; it is
raised in glory. It is sown in weakness,
raised in power. It is sown a 'natural' body,
raised a spiritual body. If there is such a
thing as a 'natural' body, then there is also
such a thing as a spiritual body. So it is
written, 'the first human being [Adam]
became a living "nature".' But the last
Adam became a life-giving spirit. The order
was not, first the spiritual, then the
'natural', but the other way round: first the
'natural' then the spiritual. The first human
being was from the soil, earthy. The second

> human being was from heaven. As was
> the earthy one, so are those who are of
> the earth; as was the heavenly one,
> so are those who are of heaven.
> And just as once we wore the likeness
> of the earthy one, so we shall also wear
> the likeness of the heavenly one.

It is very important to say here that this is not easy to understand, and so we must not leap to conclusions about what it might mean. It is also worth remembering that the people in Corinth whom Paul is addressing may well have understood more than we do of what they were hearing, since he says at the beginning of chapter 15 that he is only reminding them of what he has already preached.

Can we say anything with confidence here? Firstly, Paul clearly thinks that the Corinthians may have had a difficulty, one which we share, if we are honest, in what it could possibly mean for bodies to be raised from the dead. They knew, perhaps more directly than we do, that dead bodies start rather rapidly to decompose.

Secondly, Paul is clearly talking of two different kinds of 'body', and perhaps of two different kinds of existence. To translate these two, I have used the not altogether satisfactory pairing of 'natural' against 'spiritual'; and the speech marks round 'natural' are meant to draw your attention to the fact that it is a somewhat speculative translation. The word in Greek is *psychikos*, and you can see that it is connected with the word *psyche*, which means something like 'soul', 'life' or 'life-force'. Here it is opposed to 'spirit' and 'spiritual', and the Corinthians may, as I say, have understood better than we do what Paul meant by this opposition. It may be the same disjunction that elsewhere he calls 'spirit' and 'flesh', which is humanity as, respectively, open to God and closed to God. So we are talking of two forms of existence, that which comes from Adam, possibly corrupted by disobedience, and that which Jesus gives us, because of his obedience. One ends in death, and the other ends in Resurrection.

We have always to remember that Paul is dealing with something very new, and is reaching for vocabulary to point to the unimaginable reality of what God has done in Jesus. If we do not follow him, that is not something to wonder at; and we need a certain humility, and an absolute refusal to cram Paul into a systematic theology that may simply not have been his intention.

The other passage is from Romans 5 (12–14), where Paul is trying to give his Roman hearers a sense of the grounds for their confidence in what God has done in Christ.

> Because of this, as through a single human
> being, Sin entered the world, and through
> Sin, Death; and so Death reached to all
> human beings, insofar as all sinned. For up
> to the time of Law, Sin was in the world;
> but Sin was not counted up when there was
> no Law.

> However, Death was King from Adam until Moses, and reigned over those who had sinned in the likeness of Adam's transgression. And Adam is the likeness of the one who was to come.

Whole libraries have been written on this passage, and the phrase that I have translated, with deceptive simplicity, as 'insofar as', has been understood in at least 13 ways. So we must not be too hasty in pretending that we know what is going on here. Clearly, however, Paul regards Adam and Christ as somehow in parallel, although later in this chapter he will insist that what Christ achieved far outweighs the disaster that Adam brought about. Moreover it seems that Paul sees humanity as at the mercy of hostile powers called Sin and Death (and perhaps also Law); but what Jesus did was to liberate human beings from all that held them captive. Christ reversed what Adam had done; both Adam and Christ have universal significance, but their effects are asymmetrical. It is not easy for Paul to speak of these things, and very hard for us to understand.

Paul reaching for metaphors

Perhaps that is the point; Paul is grappling with a reality that is not easy to write about, and he struggles to find metaphors from his experience. Now you must never say '*only* a metaphor', for metaphors are indispensable short cuts, to point to a reality that is beyond language. One such metaphor is what we may translate as 'justification by faith'.

1. Justification by faith

At the heart of all Paul's metaphors is his insistence that what God has done in Christ is nothing to do with anything we have done or deserved. The key theological element here is God's unconditional love. Now this is something that human beings instinctively resist. We have a profound feeling that we have to *deserve* the love of God; and Paul will not allow that move. One of the metaphors by means of which he expresses this unconditionality is that of 'justification by faith', a phrase whose elucidation, sadly, has been thrown off kilter, and utterly bedevilled, by internal Christian polemics. Our instinct is to read the metaphor as drawn from the law-courts; if that were the case it would be a matter of our being found Not Guilty. The difficulty with that, of course, is that we are guilty, and so such a reading of justification involves God in a kind of legal fiction. So it is better if we read it as a matter of the faithfulness of God, who brings human beings into a relationship with himself, and keeps us there. And our task is to respond in trust, recognising that we are sinners, and that God is in charge.

2. Reconciliation

A second metaphor is drawn from the marriage tribunal, or the diplomatic world. It is that of reconciliation, and it is very prominent in 2 Corinthians, especially in the following passage:

> Everything comes from God, who has reconciled us to himself through Christ, and has given us the ministry of reconciliation, as that God was in Christ, reconciling the world to himself, not reckoning up their transgressions against them, and placing within us the message of reconciliation. So, on Christ's behalf, we are doing the work of ambassadors, as though God were begging us through you. We implore you, for Christ's sake, be reconciled to God.
>
> *2 Corinthians 5:18–20*

Once again, the image here has to do with the restoration of a relationship, between God and the created world; and Christ is the means by which this reconciliation takes place. And notice that God is not an enraged potentate, who has to be pacified; God is hard at work here, trying to bring Creation back to himself, rather vulnerably 'begging' us to be reconciled to him.

3. Adoption as 'sons'

Another metaphor that Paul uses is that of adoption. The word means 'adoption as sons', and I shall stay with that image, not out of any sense that only males may hope to enter the kingdom of God, but because 'adoption-as-son' is such a very striking idea in the legal world with which Paul was familiar. It was not something that you find in the Jewish world, and, interestingly, in the whole of the New Testament it appears only in Galatians 4:5; Romans 8:15, 23; 9:4 and Ephesians 1:5. So it is very much a Pauline image.

In Galatians, it forms part of a rather dense argument to the effect that what Jesus has done for us is to make us 'sons' of the Father, and of Abraham, just as he is. So he uses the language of Roman law to describe the status of the 'heir'. The heir is no better than a slave, and remains under the stern discipline of slaves (3:22, 24), until time laid down by the adoptive parent for him to enter adult life. Nevertheless, we are genuinely 'sons' (3:26), even if apparently 'no different from a slave' (4:1). However,

> When the fullness of time came, God sent his Son, born of a woman, born under [the slavery of] Law, in order to buy back those under [the slavery of] Law, in order that we might receive adoption as 'sons'.
>
> *Galatians 4:4–5*

One of the main themes of the letter to the Galatians is that of freedom, and you can see here how Paul works out his argument by way of the clashing of metaphors. The 'Son' is 'sent' into a condition of 'unfreedom' (born under a woman and under the Law) in order to create a situation of 'freedom' (by way of adoption as 'sons'). It is a powerful piece of writing, culminating in the assertion that,

> because you are 'sons', God sent the Spirit
> of his Son into our hearts, crying *Abba*,
> 'Father'.
>
> *Galatians 4:6*

The argument is more carefully worked out in Romans 8:14–15:

> Those who are led by the Spirit of God,
> these are 'sons' of God. For you did not
> receive the spirit of slavery [to fall] back
> into fear. No – what you received was the
> Spirit of adoption as 'sons', by which we
> cry *Abba*, 'Father'.

Then in the following verses, Paul plays once more with legal language about 'children' and 'heirs', and links that to the death and Resurrection of Christ (which you can never get away from in Paul). Then comes his powerful picture of creation longing for what God was going to do in Christ *waiting for the revelation of the 'sons' of God* (8:19), and then this remarkable line,

> not only that, but we ourselves also have the
> first-fruits of the Spirit, and we groan within
> ourselves, waiting for adoption as 'sons'.
>
> *Romans 8:23*

Once again, the Spirit is a key element in our self-perception as adopted 'sons', or rather in the realisation that it has not yet quite come. It is not unlike children at boarding school longing for the end of term.

On one last occasion in the Pauline literature, the image is used. It is during the long 'blessing' in Ephesians 1:3–14, the longest sentence in the New Testament. In this sentence, the author (who if it is not Paul certainly understands Paul very well indeed) outlines in his blessing of God what God has done for us in Christ. Among many other images, we have this one:

> [God] having marked us out in advance
> for adoption as 'sons' through Jesus Christ
> for him, according to his good will, to the
> praise of his glorious grace, which he has
> given us as a free gift in the Beloved . . .
>
> *Ephesians 1:5–6*

Once again, the point is that this is not something that we can do for ourselves; we absolutely depend on God's gift.

4. Redemption

'Redemption' has become a dead metaphor. It is simply the Latin word that means 'buying back'. Paul's hearers would be familiar with this from the slave-market in town. Slaves are put up for sale, and the strong or handsome ones bought up by potential owners. Just occasionally, however, it happened that a purchaser would write out the cheque for a slave, and then give him (or her) their freedom, out of human generosity. So it was decidedly a live metaphor in that world, and we should probably make a mental resolve never to use the word again, but always speak of 'buying back'. In addition to this Hellenistic strand of meaning, the word has a Jewish resonance, for it was one of the images for what God did for the people of Israel in Egypt. So at Deuteronomy 7:8 (to take an example at random, from one of Paul's favourite books) you read:

> YHWH brought you out with a powerful
> hand, and ransomed you from the house of
> slavery, from the hand of Pharaoh, king of
> Egypt *(compare 9:26; 15:15).*

This idea of redemption is also a matter for quiet confidence in the Psalms (25:22; 31:5) and the metaphor is quite prominent in Second Isaiah, another favoured passage for Paul (see Isaiah 43:1, 14; 44:22–24, a hymn to God as Redeemer; 51:11; 52:3).

Paul uses this idea at a key moment in his presentation of the argument at Romans 3:24:

> justified as a free gift by his grace through
> the redemption that is in Christ Jesus.

Here there are no less than four ways of expressing the unconditionality of what God has done, 'justified', 'free gift', 'grace', and 'redemption'. Scholars also point out that there is a similar root, which means to 'buy' or 'buy back', used in 1 Corinthians 6:20 and 7:23 (where, significantly, the context is that of slaves and the possibility of getting their freedom), and Galatians 3:13; 4:5. So it is a telling metaphor, this of redemption, and needs to have the life blown back into it.

5. Consecration and washing

Finally, here are three further metaphors, all of which are found in 1 Corinthians 6:11, after Paul has just offered a long list of those persons of unsavoury morality who will not inherit the kingdom of God:

> And some of you were all these things. But instead, you were washed, instead, you were consecrated, instead, you were justified in the name of the Lord Jesus Christ, and in the Spirit of our God.

Each of these metaphors is expressed in the passive voice (possibly because the Corinthians, as we shall see in the next chapter, were a bit over-inclined to pat themselves on the back for their spiritual progress, forgetting that it was all God's gift to them). One of them is our old friend 'justified'; but the other two come respectively from the laundry, or possibly that great institution of Hellenistic society, the public baths, and from the Temple worship. Notice that all three of these metaphors take his Corinthian hearers back to their first encounter with the gospel; so this is not their final state (he is still reproving them for their worldliness, and their tendency to take each other to court).

Conclusion

So there you have it. The heart of Paul's understanding of what God did for us in Jesus is that it was all 'free gift', or 'grace'. The other keyword here is of course 'love', to which Paul devotes a very impressive hymn in 1 Corinthians 13. And there is the clue: what Christ did for us is the outworking of a quite undeserved love. What is wrong with the Law, for Paul, is quite simply that it is not Jesus Christ, with whom Paul is so utterly in love.

Which of Paul's metaphors in your view best describes what Jesus has done for us?
Is it important to notice that they are metaphors?
What do you think Jesus has done for us?

Five

Paul on building the Christian Community

The situation in this country today

Christianity is sometimes supposed by its enemies, and perhaps by some of its adherents, to be lived in an unreal, other-worldly Utopia. Paul would have no patience with any such attitude. He was very much an inhabitant of the real world, lived with his eyes open, and wrote letters because the groups of Christians that he had started, or with whom he wished to become acquainted, had real problems in that real world.

So it may be important for you, before you start reading this chapter, to reflect on the situation in the country where you are reading this book, or the country that you know best. What are the key features of that country? What is its situation at present, socially, politically, economically? What aspects of the situation most affect those who attempt to live out the Christian gospel in it? That is something that only you can do; but it is important that you do it, to try to get a grip of what the Spirit may be saying in your situation.

The situation in the Corinth that Paul knew

Have a look at the map of Corinth below and its surroundings (you may find useful here an excellent book by Jerome Murphy-O'Connor OP, *St Paul's Corinth*, which sets the Corinthian letters as far as possible in their original context).

Corinth had a privileged situation between east and west. It sits at the top of the Peloponnese, what Paul and the Romans called Achaea, linked to Athens and Northern Greece by the narrow strip of land known as the Isthmus of Corinth. So narrow is it that at least since the days of Periander in the eighth century BC there had been plans to dig a navigable channel across the Isthmus; but nothing came of the canal until the end of the nineteenth century AD, apart from an overland passage called the Diolcos, a pathway laid out with timber across which it was possible to drag small ships. The fact was that the Greeks were not as skilled at navigation as some of their successors, and in any case, the long journey south, round the jagged ends of the Peloponnese (look at the map, and you will see what I mean) could be quite a hazardous one.

So most ships, if they were coming from the east (from the Black Sea, for example), with timber or corn or spices, would unload at Cenchreae, the easternmost port, and then transfer their cargo onto wagons for transport through Corinth and on to Lechaeum in the west. Naturally, they would pay taxes at every point, especially since the road to Lechaeum was protected by stout walls against hijackers (thefts of valuable freight are not the invention of our century). So Corinth became a very wealthy city. It was also thoroughly cosmopolitan, as you would expect of such a place; and there was a great population of slaves and of ex-slaves

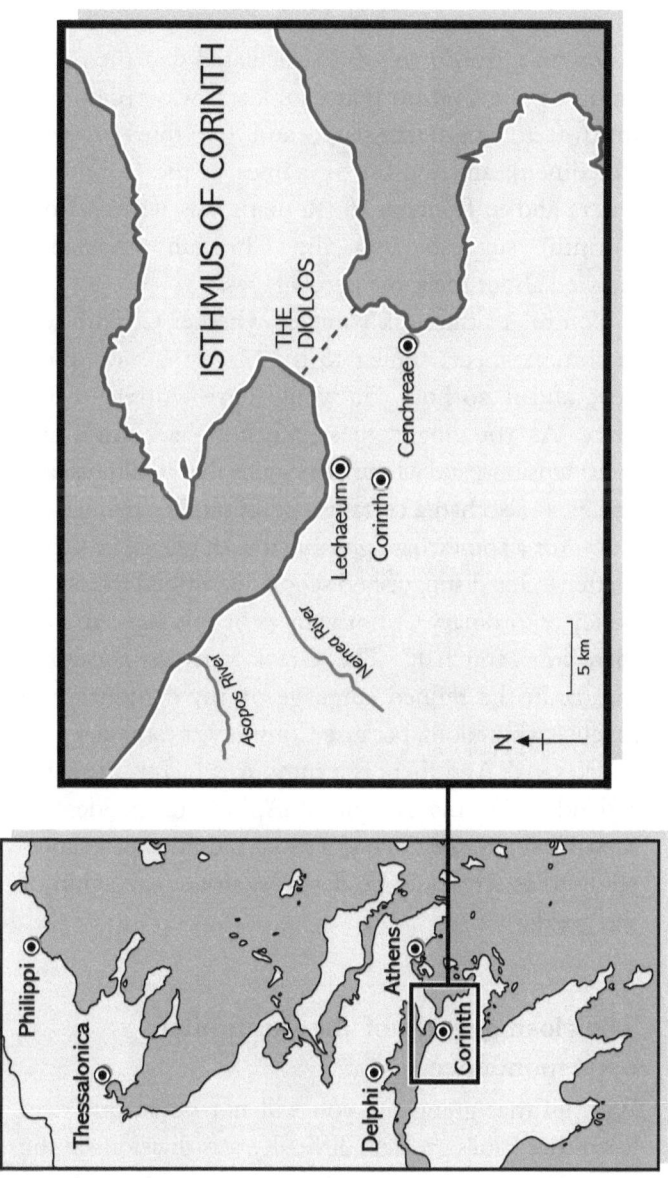

(known as 'freedmen'). It is calculated that the population of the Corinth that Paul knew was about one-third free, one-third slave, and one-third ex-slave (freedmen); and the list of names in the Corinthian letters and in Romans 16 (Romans was written from Corinth) suggests that the Christian population showed about the same percentages.

You might then ask yourself whether Corinth was in some respects similar to the place that you know best, and if so how you would have written to that place. As you might guess, Corinth had social and racial tensions, and all the difficulties that wealth usually brings. It also had a certain reputation, like many such cities, for a somewhat light touch with regard to sexual matters. One distinguished scholar described the sexual policy of ordinary Corinthians as 'if you have an itch, then you scratch it'. The Greek verb *korinthiazomai* means, in the refined language of my dictionary, 'to practice whoredom, because Corinth was famous for its courtesans'. And there is a rumour, which is probably a slander, that the Temple of Aphrodite (goddess of sexual love) in Corinth had a thousand ritual prostitutes ready to assist would-be devotees in their worship of the goddess.

The closing words of the Corinthian correspondence

With all that going on, you will not be surprised to learn that Paul's greatest difficulty was divisions in the community. The last words of 2 Corinthians have turned into a prayer that is well-known to Christians.

> The grace of Our Lord Jesus Christ, and
> the love of God, and the fellowship of the
> Holy Spirit [be] with you all.
>
> *2 Corinthians 13:13*

That word 'fellowship' is key here. It was a very important idea for Paul, and has a range of possible meanings. It means things like 'partnership', 'communion', 'union'. The Greek word for it is *koinonia*, and sometimes I like to think of it as 'solidarity'; and it was the word employed by Paul at Romans 15:26 to refer to the collection for the impoverished fellow Christians in Jerusalem, a matter very dear to Paul's heart. Sadly, though, the Corinthians never attained the *koinonia* that Paul had been hoping for; and half a century later, 1 Clement, written from Rome, indicates that the Corinthians are still at each other's throats. So Paul's two surviving letters to Corinth are written into a real situation in the real world, and we need to read them in the light of that reality (and our own, of course).

The problems at Corinth

The problems at Corinth were very much those of our own day, therefore, and if it all feels dreadfully familiar to you, then you should not be dispirited, but cheered; for it probably means that Paul is speaking your language. It is also a useful reminder that we humans do not change very much, and that the early years of the Christian church were not the blissful period of loving harmony that we sometimes suppose. As you look at the problems, just see whether you recognise them from your community, whether Christian or not, and see how Paul handles them. Could he help you today?

1. Divisions, divisions, divisions

The heart of the matter, and, in a way, the burden of the whole letter, is the wretched divisions that so afflicted them. It is a familiar, if depressing, saga to those who are involved in Christian communities, but it happens. Since Corinth was the kind of place that it is, we should not be surprised; but then look at the place where you are living today, and recognise the same syndrome. Look at how the letter starts. As usual, Paul gives thanks to God. His gratitude is, appropriately enough, for what is happening in Corinth (1:4–9); but you will notice that Paul uses here a number of passive verbs, or nouns indicating God's action (**marked in bold**) to make it clear that none of this is the Corinthians' doing:

> I give thanks to my God all the time, with regard to you, at the grace of God that **has been given to you** in Christ Jesus, because **you have** in every respect **been enriched** in him, in all rhetoric and all 'knowledge',

> as the testimony of Christ **has been
> confirmed** in you, so that you
> **are not deprived** of any **free gift**,
> but await the **revelation of Our Lord
> Jesus Christ, who will confirm** you
> to the end irreproachable on the day
> of Our Lord Jesus Christ. **God is faithful**,
> through whom **you have been called**
> into the *koinonia* of his Son, Jesus Christ
> our Lord.

Paul is very delicately reminding them that their spiritual gifts and graces are not their own doing, but are given to them by God. At the same time, you might count the number of times that Paul mentions the name of his beloved Jesus (or Christ or Christ Jesus) in the first ten verses. Here, too, there is another reminder of the way out of their problem: eyes on Jesus!

Then he starts (verse 10) to deal with their problems, but without actually saying so; he asks them:

> through the name of our Lord Jesus, all to
> say the same thing, and for there not to be
> divisions among you.

The word for 'divisions' is *schismata*, which is what scissors do. Half of all the New Testament uses of this noun appear in 1 Corinthians, significantly enough (though it is only fair to admit that it is just three out of six!). It is worth saying at this point that the Corinthians have written him a letter, and they will be expecting him to answer the various queries that they have; but they are going to have to wait until the beginning of chapter 7 for any answers to be given. Instead, Paul deals with the real questions that they should have had:

> ... there are quarrels among you! I'm
> talking about this: each of you is saying,
> 'I'm a Paul-man'; 'I'm for Apollos'; 'I'm
> for Kephas'. Well – I'm a Christ-man!

As we have already said, there is no punctuation in our Greek, so we do not know how this would have been read to the church in Corinth. I have taken a view, which is defensible but cannot be proved beyond doubt, that there are three parties in Corinth, the Paul group, the Apollos group, and (perhaps – or is Paul being diplomatic here?) a Kephas or Peter group. Then he makes his grim little joke, and reminds them where their eyes should be: on Christ. Other scholars, it must be admitted, think of four groups, the fourth being a 'Christ group', and have some ingenious speculations about how the groups might be different. It may be worth saying just a little bit about Apollos. We hear of him in Acts 18:24–19:1, where we learn that:

> ... a certain Jew called Apollos,
> an Alexandrian by race, a cultured man,
> turned up in Ephesus. He was very good at
> the Scriptures. Now he had been given
> instruction in the Lord's Way; he was

> zealous in the Spirit, and started teaching
> accurately all about Jesus; but he
> only knew the baptism of John!
>
> He began to be very frank in the
> synagogue; when Priscilla and Aquila heard
> him, they took hold of him, and gave him a
> more accurate presentation of The Way.
>
> Since he wanted to go to Achaea,
> the brothers and sisters gave him
> encouragement, and wrote to the disciples
> to give him hospitality. He turned up
> and was of assistance to those who had
> come to faith through grace. For he would
> vigorously and publicly refute the Jews,
> demonstrating on the basis of Scripture
> that Jesus was indeed the Messiah.

You can see why there might have been tension with Paul. Apollos was eloquent, and some complained that Paul was not (2 Corinthians 10:10). Apollos had come fairly recently to a belief in Jesus ('The Way'); he came from Alexandria, where among both Jews and Christians there was a very distinctive tradition of rich Scripture-interpretation. He was a zealot, with all the naïve enthusiasm of the convert, and evidently did not get it all right, and was only baptised after the manner of John, presumably not in the triune name of 'Father, Son and Holy Spirit'. Apollos' heart was clearly in the right place, but he may have started to attract people to his way of talking about Jesus, and in consequence, even unwittingly, divided the Corinthian community after he journeyed there from Ephesus. Paul's friends Priscilla and Aquila seem to have been helpful here. But divisions there undoubtedly were in this Corinthian church.

2. Wisdom and knowledge

Two words that you will often see in the Corinthian correspondence are 'wisdom' (*sophia* in Greek) and 'knowledge' (*gnosis*). These two qualities were highly valued by educated Greeks. Now at least some of the Corinthian Christians regarded themselves as highly educated, and wanted Paul to provide evidence to the intellectual leaders of Corinth that Christians were as good as anybody else when it came to *sophia* and *gnosis*. They also wanted Paul to demonstrate another quality that they looked for in their intellectual leaders, which they called *logos*. This means 'word', but can also mean 'eloquence', and in 1 Corinthians, I suspect that Paul uses it to mean 'rhetoric', and *sophia* to mean 'cleverness', both of them in a pejorative sense. As I indicated above, there had been complaints about Paul's lack of rhetoric (2 Corinthians 10:9–11; and see 11:5–6, 16). Probably some of the Christians of Corinth wanted Paul to be the 'spin-doctor', or 'sophist' that Corinth needed if it was to compete with other cities. Christians are not immune to the desire to be 'intellectually respectable' or even acceptable to the chattering classes, an aim that Paul would have regarded as contemptible.

3. Incest

Incest is, of course, a problem in our culture; it is not simply an ancient, nor simply a rural vice. Most cases of sexual abuse of children take place within the family. And here in Corinth there was an example that clearly horrified Paul, with his strong Jewish background in sexual morality. This is what he had to say about that:

> It is even said that there is sexual immorality among you! And sexual immorality of a kind that is unheard of even among the Gentiles, that a man has his father's wife! You people are so puffed up. Shouldn't you rather be sorry for it? The person committing this crime should be taken from your midst . . .
>
> *1 Corinthians 5:1–2*

Read the following six verses to see the severe punishment that Paul imposes on the miscreant. One thing that is clear is that Paul subscribes to the philosophy that 'one rotten apple infects the whole barrel' (see verses 6–7), and that to have someone like that as part of the body of Christ in Corinth is dangerous for the entire group of Christians.

4. Litigation

Not only that, but the Christians in Corinth were taking each other to court! Paul is incredulous:

> One of you has the nerve, when he has an
> issue with someone else, to go to court
> with the unrighteous and not with the
> saints ... I am speaking to put you to
> shame. Don't you have anyone 'wise/clever'
> enough, who can make a decision about a
> fellow Christian? Instead, Christians have
> lawsuits against other Christians – and
> in the presence of unbelievers!
>
> It is already a defeat for you that
> you have lawsuits against each other.
> Shouldn't you rather suffer injustice?
> Instead, you people are committing
> injustice and deprivation and you do it
> to fellow Christians!
>
> *1 Corinthians 6:1–8*

For Paul, if you are acting in this way, you have simply not understood what it means to be a Christian, that we actually belong together in *koinonia*. And the Corinthians were incredibly complacent about it all. Regrettably, such actions have not been unknown among Christians in the centuries since Paul wrote to his Corinthians.

5. Freedom

One of the underlying themes of the Letter to the Galatians (which some scholars regard as Paul's first surviving epistle) is 'freedom'. He thought that those Galatians who were being persuaded by the arguments of those who came from Jerusalem and wanted to return to strict observance of Jewish Law, were simply turning their backs on the freedom that Christ came to offer them. Have a look at Galatians 2:4 and 5:1, 13, to see how Paul emphasises this theme in that letter.

So the chances are that when he came to Corinth for the first time, to a rather different, largely Gentile, group, he may have announced that he was bringing a gospel of 'freedom'. If that is so, he soon learnt the mistake. The Corinthians were closer in mood to 1960s hippies than to more rigidly restrained religious groupings (against which the aforesaid hippies might be thought to have been in revolt). So if he did preach a message of liberty in Corinth, they may have shouted 'Whoopee! Now we can do what we like.' It looks as though they quoted back to him a slogan that he may have used in describing this gospel of freedom. The Greek slogan is *panta exesti*, which you might translate as 'everything is permitted', or, in 1960's-speak, 'do your own thing'. So at 1 Corinthians 6:12, you hear Paul having that slogan quoted back to him:

> 'Everything is permitted.'

Then he responds:

> Yes – but not everything is advantageous. Everything is indeed 'permitted', but that doesn't mean that I'll surrender my freedom to anything.

The last line here actually continues the quotation from them, and might be better translated as:

> that doesn't mean that anybody is going to 'permit' me

which brings out Paul's insistent repetition of the 'all things are permitted' slogan which the Corinthians have flung in his face.

And he then goes on to demonstrate why they can't simply 'do their own thing' in the matter of sexual morality. Paul may have rued the day when, in a city like Corinth he told them 'everything is permitted', and had to say, 'but I didn't mean *that*!'

He quotes the slogan again, at 10:23. *Everything is permitted,* and then refines it twice more:

> Yes – but not everything is advantageous.
> 'Everything is permitted' – but not
> everything builds up.

Here, with the motif of 'upbuilding' or, literally 'house-building' (which comes into English, via Latin, as 'edifying'), he is on to a very important theme in the letter. Back in chapter 3:9c–17, when trying to explain what the function of Paul and Apollos is, he used the image of a building, and the verb 'build on top of'. You can feel Paul moving towards the answer to the problem of the divisions that came from an exaggerated understanding of Christian freedom. But we are getting ahead of ourselves, and that must wait for our treatment of the answers that Paul produces. He never, however, abandoned his insight that Christ's gospel is one of freedom, even for Corinthians. So at 2 Corinthians 3:17 we overhear him telling the Corinthians:

> The Lord is the Spirit; and where the Lord's
> Spirit is, there is freedom.

6. A host of other issues

There were several other neuralgic points in that Corinthian church; for once you start being divided, almost any issue will do as a peg on which to hang your divisions.

Some such issues may have reared their ugly heads in communities known to you, such as sex and the role of women. We shall be looking at these two in later chapters. Then there was the difficult question of food sacrificed to idols, which is perhaps not a major problem for contemporary Christian communities (although they might have to examine themselves regarding their attitudes to the false gods of our time). Paul considers this issue in 1 Corinthians 8–10; and the principles he outlines there are still valid today. See especially his concluding reflections (10:23–24):

> Yes – but not everything is advantageous.
> 'Everything is permitted' – but not
> everything builds up. Let no one look for
> their own interests; no – look for other
> people's.

Then, in verses 25–30, he offers some reflections that remain helpful with regard to conscience and the difficult question of eating food bought in the market, a cheap way, in that world, of getting hold of necessary protein. Then he concludes:

> So – whether you eat or whether you drink, or whether you do anything at all, do everything for God's glory. Don't be a source of offence to Jews or Gentiles or the church of God, just as I please everybody in every respect, not seeking my own advantage, but the advantage of the majority, so that they may be saved.
> Be imitators of me, as I also am an imitator of Christ.
> *1 Corinthians 10:31–11:1*

You might think how you would apply these principles to the resolution of any contemporary issue in the churches. And there are other problems that Paul has to deal with, such as that of noisy and undisciplined liturgies which he wrestles with in chapters 10–14; or getting the Resurrection wrong (mainly by not believing in it – chapter 15). Either of these might be a current problem.

7. Social tensions

We indicated above that the Corinthian community as a whole was multicultural, and it looks as though the band of Christians in that noisy city was a reflection of the wider population. It can be very enriching to have several cultures feeding into a group; but it can also be a dreadful source of tension. And Paul, it seems, had heard of one example of the tensions. It concerned (of all things!) the Eucharist. Devastatingly, he tells them off for it:

> ... when you come together, it is not for the better, but for the worse. For in the first place, I gather that when you come together as a church, there are divisions among you! And, in part, I can credit it; for you need to have sects among you, so that the tried and tested can show their worth among you. So when you come together in the same place, it is **not** to eat the Lord's Supper! Because each of you takes your own supper, ahead of the time of eating; and some go hungry, while others are drunk! Don't you have houses to eat and drink in? Do you despise the church of God, and cause embarrassment to the have-nots?
>
> *1 Corinthians 11:17b–22*

Paul is clearly very cross here, because as far as he is concerned the church should not be divided in this way, along class lines. Probably what has happened is that those who were well-to-do could come to the gathering any time they pleased, and perhaps these more affluent ones would be more congenial for the relatively wealthy owner of a house large enough to contain all the community; while the poor, and, worse still, the slaves, have jobs that keep them until late. So Paul tells them that their meal 'is not . . . the Lord's Supper', which must have been a very considerable shock to them.

As always, Paul goes back to Jesus, and, as so often, we must be grateful to those who annoyed him, because they forced out of him something that we might not have had if he had not lost his temper, evidence of what he believed about the Eucharist, namely that it goes back to Jesus, and that it is for everybody. So he writes to correct them:

> For I received from the Lord, what I also
> passed on to you, that the Lord Jesus, on
> the night on which he was betrayed, took
> bread, and after giving thanks, broke [it]
> and said, 'This is my body, which is for you.
> Do this for my remembrance.' In just the
> same way, with the cup, after supper, saying,
> 'This cup is the new covenant in my blood.
> Do this, whenever you drink it, for my
> remembrance.' For as often as you eat this
> bread and drink the cup, you are
> proclaiming the Lord's death, until he comes.
> *1 Corinthians 11:23–27*

This is evidently Christian tradition, and we are glad to have it; but notice why it is quoted at this point.

It is in order to find a solution to the tensions within the Christian community, by forcing them to look once more at what Jesus did, especially on that momentous night, and so adapt their Eucharistic practice.

8. Mistrust

At the bottom of it all, though, was the poison of mistrust that had seeped into the community, affecting their relationship with each other, and their relationship with Paul. Here is a very telling instance of it:

> With regard to the collection for the saints,
> as I have instructed the churches of
> Galatia, you are to do likewise: every
> Sunday, let each of you set aside, storing up
> whatever you have managed to earn, so that
> when I come, then the accounts can be
> drawn up. And when I am with you, the
> people whom **you** approve, I'll send them
> on their way with letters, to take your free
> gift to Jerusalem. And if it is appropriate
> for me to go as well, they will travel with me.
> *1 Corinthians 16:1–4*

The 'collection' for the impoverished Christians of Jerusalem was a matter of great importance for Paul, and it turned out that the Corinthians were readier to talk than to put their hands in their pockets, for quite a sizeable chunk of 2 Corinthians (chapters 8 and 9) is taken up with that issue. With regard to the situation in Corinth, we may notice, first, the appeal to other churches (Galatia – the Corinthians thought they were superior to these Turks). Second, they apparently do not sufficiently trust each other to bring the money along to the assembly on Sundays, but are to keep the money at home. Third, Paul insists on proper accounting. Fourth, he is clearly aware that they do not wholly trust him, and accepts that the people who are to take the money to Jerusalem are to be those chosen, not by himself, but by the Corinthians. Finally, he is not even insisting that he must travel with the delegates; he is apparently leaving that decision to them.

So the poison of mistrust has gone deep into the community.

Paul's solutions to the problems

How does Paul deal with the difficulties? (Or, rather, difficulty: the basic problem in Corinth was the fact that they were a divided community.) There are various ways of looking at what he does in 1 Corinthians, but I should like to suggest to you that he offers three answers, then that he uses three techniques to keep them in order, and, finally, that he makes one very important point that we might usefully reflect upon today.

1. Three answers

The first answer to their problem is, frankly, the cross. As always, Paul's approach is to insist that people keep their eyes on Jesus, and here he is able to point to himself, though I think that we can acquit him of arrogance on that account:

> And when I came to you, brothers and
> sisters, I did not come in any pre-eminence
> of rhetoric, or in human cleverness, when
> I proclaimed God's mystery to you. For
> I decided to have no 'knowledge' among
> you except Jesus Christ – and him crucified.
> And I came to you in weakness and fear,
> and in much trembling. And my rhetoric,
> and my proclamation, was not a matter of
> spin-doctoring cleverness; it was a matter
> of showing the Spirit and power.
>
> *1 Corinthians 2:1–4*

Notice here how Paul uses the technical terms that the Corinthians have apparently been brandishing at him: rhetoric (*logos*), cleverness (*sophia*), and knowledge (though here he actually uses the verb, not the noun *gnosis*). As far as we can tell from the evidence in Acts 17–18, Paul arrived in the decidedly unpromising city of Corinth straight from a minor disaster in Athens, where his carefully crafted speech at the Areopagus had broken up in hoots of derisive laughter when he started talking about the Resurrection (Acts 17:32–33). So in Corinth he is going to lay all the emphasis on Christ crucified, which, he insists in the rest of chapter 2, is a matter of divine wisdom quite different from mere human cleverness by which the Corinthians are setting so much store.

The second answer is to try to persuade the Corinthians to see themselves as a 'body', every part of which belongs together. This was a common idea in the political theory of the day; but I know of no one who managed the idea of the body with such humour and originality as Paul here. The passage comes in chapter 12, where he is trying to deal with the difficult question of their undisciplined liturgies, but it works also for the stark fact of their divisions. This is how Paul presents the notion of the church as the body of Christ:

> You see, just as the body is a single entity,
> with many members, so it is with Christ.
> For by a single Spirit, every one of us
> was baptised into one body, Jews or Gentiles,
> slaves or free men and women, and we
> were all given to drink of the single Spirit.
> The body is not one member, but several.
> *1 Corinthians 12:12–27*

Then Paul gives some mildly comical examples of how the foot might make a bid for independence on the grounds of not being a hand, or the ear, on the grounds of not being an eye; and he even brings in the head and the sense of smell (15–17). Then he continues:

> As it is, God has placed the limbs, each one
> of them, just as he wanted, in the body. If
> they were all just one member, where would

the body be? As it is, there are many limbs
and a single body (18–20).

However the real problem at Corinth was not merely that they regarded the other with suspicion, but also that they thought some members of the body were inferior to others. Paul makes it clear that this is not God's view:

> The members of the body that seem to be
> weaker are necessary; the bits of the body
> that we think are less honourable, these are
> the very ones to which we give more
> abundant honour; and our indecent bits
> receive more abundant decency, while our
> decent bits have no need of it. No – it was
> God who composed the body, giving more
> abundant honour to the part that lacked it,
> so that there might not be a division *[that
> word again]* in the body, but all the members
> might care for each other . . . You are the
> Body of Christ, and in part its members.
> *1 Corinthians 12:22–27*

To get the force of what Paul is saying here, it has been necessary to translate the word for 'limbs', parts of the body, as 'members', which, presumably under the pressure of this text, as the Latin word for limbs, has come to take on its present English meaning. And I have likewise translated the word for 'one' as 'single', to stress the point that Paul is making.

Then, almost immediately, there comes a third answer. Like the image of the Body of Christ, it belongs in the context, but also it can stand alone (which is why you hear it read at so many weddings); and it spoke profoundly to the divisions among the Corinthians, even if they were not listening. This third answer is, of course, the great hymn to love in chapter 13. It is an odd passage, in some ways, and it interrupts slightly the flow between chapters 12 and 14, but it is clearly written with the Corinthians in mind. We shall not lay it out in full here, as it will appear in a subsequent chapter, but notice the following elements in it.

First, it is aimed directly at those Corinthians who had the gift of tongues and prophecy and heavenly revelations (*the tongues of human beings and of angels*, verse 1, *prophecy and mysteries,* verse 2); and Paul uses an image from Corinth itself when he speaks of *echoing bronze and clashing cymbal*; for there was mined in the area a kind of bronze that was ideally suited to the making of cymbals. There is, inevitably, a reference to *gnosis*. Then comes a description of what love is like (some people see this as Paul's portrait of his beloved Jesus), including the fact that *it is kindly* (and the Greek word here would have sounded like 'behaves like Christ') and *it is not puffed up*, which, as we shall see in a minute, Paul thought could be said about his opponents in Corinth. Then, in verses 8–12, comes a meditation on knowledge (note that word once more), in which he makes it quite clear that the *gnosis* to which the Corinthians were laying claim is very far from being perfect *(the things of an infant)*. Finally, we hear the towering sentence with which the hymn ends, and which Paul doubtless hoped might finally reduce their quarrelling to silence:

> As it is, there remain faith, hope, love, these three things: and the greatest of these is love.

2. Three techniques for keeping them in order

Paul does a number of things to make it clear that he is not going to give in to these rebels. The first thing that he does is to face the facts. We have already seen him do this with regard to the fault line between the Paul-party and the Apollos-party earlier in the letter; and in chapter 3 he examines that fault line, and explains what the function of Paul and Apollos is. He offers three images. The Corinthian church is seen first as a garden (3:4–9), then as a building (9–15), and finally, by an imperceptible slide from the notion of building, as a Temple (16–17). Then he sums up in a characteristic passage. Notice how he slows down towards the end, as he reaches the name of his beloved Jesus, who forms the zenith of the passage.

> Let no one deceive themselves: if someone thinks that they are clever among you in this age, let them become stupid, in order to become clever. For the cleverness of this world is stupidity in God's eyes. For it is written, 'the one who catches the clever in

> their craftiness', and again, 'The Lord
> knows the thoughts of the clever, that they
> are useless'. So let no one go boasting
> about human beings; for everything
> belongs to you, whether Paul or Apollos, or
> Kephas, or the universe, or life, or death, or
> things present, or things to come, all is
> yours, and you are Christ's, and Christ
> is God's.
>
> *1 Corinthians 3:18–22*

Do you see how neatly he turns the point? Paul uses those important terms of 'clever' and 'cleverness' ('wise' and 'wisdom'), and robs them of all significance by dismissing talk of them and of the party leaders as 'boasting'; and, as always with Paul, he brings the whole episode back to Christ and to God, setting it all in the context in which it belongs.

Secondly, Paul is not afraid to put the Corinthians firmly in their place. Listen to this, and imagine what those rather complacent Christians felt as this was read out in their assembly:

> For look at your calling, brothers and
> sisters; because not many of you were
> 'clever' (according to the flesh), not many
> of you were powerful, not many of you
> were nobly born. No – God selected the
> morons of this world, to put the 'clever' to
> shame; and God chose the weaklings of the
> world, to put the strong to shame; and the

unborn of the world, and those regarded
with contempt God chose, those that are
not, in order to cancel out those that are,
to prevent flesh boasting before God.

1 Corinthians 1:26–29

This is strong language; and we can see something of the same at 3:1–4:

Brothers and sisters, I was unable to talk to
you as spiritual people; no – I [had to talk
to you] as flesh people, as infants in Christ.
I gave you milk to drink, not [proper] food,
because you were not yet up to it. And even
now, you aren't up to it; you see, when there
is jealousy and quarrelling among you,
aren't you being flesh people? Aren't you
behaving just like human beings? When
someone says 'I'm a Paul-man', and
someone else says, 'I'm for Apollos', aren't
you just being human beings?

We may imagine some embarrassment and irritation in the assembly as this was read out to them. They will also have been waiting for Paul to answer their letter to him, and expecting that it would come fairly soon; instead, it is not until chapter 7:1 that they hear him grudgingly contriving a reply: *Now – as for your letter . . .*

Thirdly, Paul is unafraid to employ the weapons of sarcasm (4:8, for example), physical threats (4:21; and would you be confident in alleging that Paul was not serious in threatening them with corporal punishment?), and anger (9:1). You may reflect that Paul must have been very confident of the affection of his Corinthians to take risks of that sort, although 2 Corinthians indicates that they did not react very well to the first letter.

3. 'Upbuilding' against inflatable toads
A final tool in Paul's armoury in his dealing with this very lively, if not always tractable, community may need us to pause and reflect a bit. It is the distinction that he makes between what he is trying to do for this broken church, to 'upbuild' it, and what his opponents are up to. For he calls them 'puffed-up'. You may care to reflect here on those toads in the rainforests of South America which defend themselves against predators by swelling up and frightening them off; but in fact, though they may look formidable, they are rather insubstantial, and can be pricked, like balloons, with a pin.

At the end of his treatment of himself and Apollos, in which he defines them as 'servants of Christ', Paul says (1 Corinthians 4:6):

> I have applied this image to myself and
> Apollos . . . so as to avoid one of us getting
> 'puffed up' against the other.

Later in the same chapter he employs the idea again, this time with regard to some of his opponents, in the context of his commendation of Timothy, and he says):

> Some of you, under the supposition that
> I was not coming to you, have got 'puffed
> up', but I'm coming to you soon enough,
> and then I shall know with regard to the
> 'puffed up people', not [how good] their
> rhetoric [is], but [how much] substance
> [they have].
>
> *1 Corinthians 4:18–19*

And when he starts to deal with the question of incest, he is savage with them for not having done something about the 'rotten apple' (5:2):

> You people are 'puffed up' – shouldn't you
> rather be in mourning?

The only other place in the New Testament where this word is used is Colossians 2:18, so it looks as though it is of particular importance for what Paul saw as going wrong in Corinth. There are two final uses of it, where we may get a clue as to what he was trying to do, and its wider application to Paul beyond Corinth.

The first is at 8:1, when he turns to dealing with the question that they have raised about the permissibility of eating food offered to idols. It is hard to be sure, but it looks as though they have presented the problem in terms of their knowledge (*gnosis*); and Paul wants them to see that there is another value besides that of knowledge.

> Now, with regard to food offered to idols,
> we know that we all have *gnosis*. *Gnosis*
> 'puffs up' – but love **builds up**.

Here is the point; for Paul, if you live in Christ, you do so in community; therefore one of the signs that we should be looking for is that of love, a quality that is very much there in Paul, but not overly noticeable among his Corinthians. Knowledge, by contrast, is not very important, as far as he is concerned, and so he continues (8:2–3):

> If someone thinks that they know
> something, they don't yet know as they
> should know. But if someone loves God,
> then they are known by God.
> *1 Corinthians 8:2–3*

Do you see how neatly he redirects their ideas, away from 'knowledge' and towards love? Now listen to this phrase from the hymn to love in chapter 13, as he describes how love operates (verses 4–5):

> Love is patient, is kindly, love is not jealous,
> does not bear a grudge, is not 'puffed up',
> does not behave indecently, does not seek
> what is its own, is not provoked . . .

If the Corinthians were still listening by this stage of the letter, they should have been hanging their heads in shame.

Conclusion

So building the Christian community is no easy task, and it involves keeping a clear eye, first on the reality of the situation in which you are living, and second on the person of Christ, and what it means, here and now, to live 'in Christ'. Listen now to the way in which Paul concludes the two surviving letters to the Christian community in Corinth. First, 1 Corinthians 16:19–24:

> The churches of Asia greet you. Aquila and Prisca send you many greetings in the Lord, along with the whole church in their house. All the brothers and sisters greet you. [I want you to] greet each other with a holy kiss.
>
> The greeting in *my* hand: PAUL
>
> If someone does not love the Lord, let them be anathema *('cursed' in Greek)*. Maranatha *('Our Lord has come' or 'Come Lord' in Aramaic)*. The grace of the Lord Jesus be with you. My love be with all of you in Christ Jesus.

You can see it all for yourself here: the emphasis on the fact that there are other Christians elsewhere in the world (something that the Corinthians were not all that aware of); the mention of Prisca and Aquila, whom the Corinthians knew, of course; the insistence on love and on greeting and, even, no doubt to the horror of the quarrelling Corinthians, a 'kiss'. Then Paul adds a personal touch, grabbing the pen, and writing for himself, in his own rather different and large handwriting. And the insistence of love for the Lord, the grace of Jesus, and Paul's love for them. And by now you will not be surprised that the last two words of the letter are 'Christ Jesus'.

Now look at the ending of 2 Corinthians:

> . . . for we rejoice whenever we are weak,
> but you are powerful. This is what we are
> praying for – your being made complete.
> This is why I am writing in my absence,
> so that in my presence I shan't have to deal
> with you severely (in accordance with the
> authority that the Lord has given me – for
> **upbuilding** and not for destruction). For
> the rest, brothers and sisters, rejoice, be
> made complete, be comforted, all have the
> same mindset, and the God of love and
> peace be with you. Greet each other with
> a holy kiss. All the saints are sending you
> greetings. The grace of the Lord Jesus Christ,
> and the love of God, and the solidarity
> of the Holy Spirit be with all of you.
>
> *2 Corinthians 13:9–13*

It is all there, a last desperate (and probably in the end unsuccessful) attempt to bring them to their senses, with a touch of familiar sarcasm and reproof, a mention, once more, of upbuilding, an emphasis on unanimity and getting it right. And, above all and always, his eyes are where he wishes theirs were, on God and on Jesus and on the Spirit.

What would Paul say to your city today?
Is the idea of 'upbuilding' helpful in your setting?

Six

Paul on prayer

What is prayer? There are many possible definitions, and it is a wise monastic rule to 'pray as you can, not as you can't'. The ancient catechism definition on which I was brought up was 'prayer is the raising up of the mind and heart to God'. If you do not care for the tone of that, you could call it something like 'opening up to the transcendent'. I should be inclined to make the claim, one that some readers will perhaps resist, that it is impossible for humans to attain maturity without something like prayer in their life. This claim is not essential to the argument of the present chapter, however, so I shall leave it hanging in the air.

Paul however, would, in my view, take some such line as the above, and it may be worth keeping it in mind as we go through the texts that follow. We can approach the topic by putting a series of questions to Paul. They may illuminate both Paul's approach to prayer and the anxieties of people today.

How often should we pray?

Beginners often ask about how frequently we should pray, and for Paul the answer seems to be, 'all the time'. So at 1 Thessalonians 5:16–20, we read:

> Rejoice all the time, pray without ceasing,
> give thanks in every respect. For this is

> God's will for you in Christ Jesus.
> Don't extinguish the Spirit, don't despise prophecy.

So this praying business is non-stop, as far as Paul is concerned: 'all the time' and 'without ceasing'. That may seem impossible to you; but it appears that there are some people, no doubt very advanced in prayer, who experience themselves as always 'tuned in' to God. We may also anticipate what we shall be saying later, by observing that the content of the prayer can be characterised as 'rejoicing' and 'giving thanks'. There are two other things to notice here. First, Paul clearly thinks in terms of the 'will of God'. Second, Paul gives prayer what you might call a 'proto-Trinitarian' shape. Not that Paul had ever heard of the word 'Trinity'; but certainly for him the story of God had now to include also his beloved Jesus Christ and that strange, but to Paul and his Christian groups, palpable, power to which they gave the name of Spirit.

We might further notice that human beings have a choice in the matter; it is possible for them to 'extinguish' the Spirit, as one might pour water on a fire, and that 'prophecy', to which Paul gives quite a high status, is something that humans can disdain. Underneath the whole text, however, we observe that Paul thinks that human beings can open up to the transcendent, and that it is a part of mature Christian living.

Certainly, Paul claims for himself that he goes in for uninterrupted prayer:

> I give thanks to God, whom I worship with a clear conscience (something I got from my ancestors), how I make unceasing mention of you in my prayers, night and day.
>
> *2 Timothy 1:3*

We find the same claim of 'non-stop prayer' at Romans 1:9; 12:12; 1 Corinthians 1:4; Philippians 1:3–4; 1 Thessalonians 1:2; 3:10. You might also look at Philemon 4 and compare Colossians 1:3; Ephesians 1:16; 6:18.

What should we do when we pray?

Above all, Paul wants his Christians to give thanks, and, as we have seen, he is constantly doing so himself. It is a matter of empirical observation that a stance of gratitude is quite an important element in appropriate adult maturity and balance. We have already made the point that Paul can usually be heard giving thanks very early in his letters. This is a standard example, at Romans 1:8:

> In the first place, I give thanks to my God through Jesus Christ, with regard to all of you . . .

We notice also the characteristic thanksgiving at the beginning of 1 Corinthians, suitably tailored for the situation of that divided church:

> I am always giving thanks to my God with regard to you, because of the grace of God that has been given to you in Christ Jesus . . .

(compare the 'double thanksgiving' of 1 Thessalonians 1:2; 2:13, and 2 Thessalonians 1:3; 2:13). There is also a startling outpouring of gratitude in 1 Thessalonians 3:9–10:

> . . . for what thanks can we repay to the Lord, to make up for you with all the joy with which we rejoice on your account before our God?

See also Philippians 1:3–6; Colossians 1:3 and Ephesians 1:16 for the same ebullient outpouring of gratitude. In Colossians 4:2 Paul indicates that it is not just he who has to be grateful, but his hearers also.

As well as being grateful in prayer, however, it is noticeable that Paul's Christians are also permitted to ask for things. That seems quite important, as we tend to dismiss petitionary prayer as 'infantile'. Perhaps it depends what kind of thing you are asking for. Paul has no problem, for example, in asking:

> that somehow I may some day succeed in coming to you, by God's will; for I am longing to see you . . . *Romans 1:9–11*

Likewise, he is quite candid in asking them to pray for him:

> I am imploring you, brothers and sisters,
> through our Lord Jesus Christ and through
> the love of the Spirit, to fight alongside me
> in your prayers for me to God, so that
> I may be delivered from the unbelievers in
> Judaea, and that my collection [*diakonia*]
> may turn out to be acceptable to the
> saints . . .
>
> *Romans 15:30–32*

The Ephesians are also to pray:

> . . . through all prayer and entreaty praying
> at all times in the Spirit, and staying awake
> for that purpose, in all perseverance and
> entreaty for all the saints, and on my behalf,
> that eloquence may be given me when I
> open my mouth, that I may have the
> openness to proclaim the gospel-mystery,
> for which I am an ambassador in my
> imprisonment, that in the gospel I may
> speak freely, as I ought to speak.
>
> *Ephesians 6:18–20*

Perhaps it may be worth saying something more general about this business of asking for things. Jesus included petitions for things in the prayer that he gave his disciples, but there is nothing about thanksgiving in the Lord's Prayer (although he does give thanks himself: Matthew 11:25; Luke 10:21). Jesus also instructs us to be proactive in prayer, telling us to 'ask', 'seek', 'knock' (Matthew 7:7–11; Luke 11:9–13); and experience tells us that doing these things has effects, whereas failure to do so yields nothing at all.

What happens in prayer?

For Paul, evidently, some remarkable things happen when he is praying, although he only mentions them when sufficiently annoyed (in this case by the church in Corinth: see 2 Corinthians 12:1–4):

> I have to boast. It is not to anyone's advantage; but I shall come to 'visions' and 'revelations of the Lord'. I know a person in Christ, fourteen years since (whether in the body I don't know; or out of the body, I don't know – God knows). This person was snatched up as far as the third heaven. And I know a person just like this (whether in the body or out of the body, I don't know, God knows); I know that he was snatched up into Paradise; and he heard words that can't be spoken, things that it is not permissible for a person to utter.
>
> *2 Corinthians 12:1–4*

Paul makes a pretence that he is not talking about himself, but abandons the pretence by the time he gets to verse 7, when he speaks of the famous 'thorn in the flesh'. The point as far as we are concerned is that Paul (if we are correct in reading the text in this way) had very exalted mystical experiences that changed his life. The context is one of complaints about Paul not being a real apostle, and so, reluctantly, he is driven to say something about his experiences in prayer.

And, while we are on the matter, it may be good to talk about the 'thorn in the flesh', since everyone asks what it was. There are three, perhaps four, possibilities. The one most often advanced, probably because so many exegetes have traditionally been male, is that it was a sexual temptation of some kind. There is of course no shred of evidence for this supposition. The second is that Paul was epileptic. This is a way of 'explaining' Luke's version of his encounter with Jesus: it was not the real thing, but a medical condition. Thirdly, he might well have had something wrong with his eyes. He reminds the Galatians (4:12b–15):

> You did me no wrong; you know that it was
> because of a weakness of the flesh that
> I preached the gospel to you that first time,
> and you did not disdain or 'spit out' your
> temptation in my flesh . . . I can give
> evidence on your behalf that if you could
> have, you would have dug out your eyes
> and given them to me!

So Paul may well have had an eye-infection of a painful and embarrassing sort; but we do not have any evidence. Finally, I suppose, it might not be a metaphor at all, but an actual thorn that he could not remove.

The Corinthians will have known what he was talking about; but Paul is not telling us, and there we must leave the matter, since it is Paul's prayer-life that we are talking about, not his physical, mental or moral health.

Another effect of the Christian's prayer-life that Paul appears to have known at first hand is that tangible and powerful experience to which the early Christians gave the name of 'the Spirit'. Listen to what he says to the Galatians. Angrily he demands of them:

> I just want to learn this of you: was it
> because of works of the Law that you
> received the Spirit, or because of hearing
> it in faith?
> *Galatians 3:2–3*

The point here is that it is common ground between Paul and his Galatians that they did receive the Spirit, so much so that he does not have to explain what 'receiving the Spirit' might be; they knew perfectly well what he meant. At Galatians 4:6, he makes a similar appeal to what they have in common:

> ... but because you are sons [and daughters],
> God sent the Spirit of his Son into our
> hearts, crying out, 'Abba, Father'.

And at Galatians 5:22–23, presumably, he is likewise telling them what they already know, when he speaks of the 'fruits of the Spirit':

> The fruit of the Spirit is: love, joy, peace,
> patience, kindness, goodness, faith,
> gentleness, chastity.

All this is something that Paul's Christians could detect for themselves as the effects of their prayer-life. The same is true of 'speaking in tongues', a gift on which the Corinthians so prided themselves. In the context of an attempt to get some order into their liturgical behaviour, and presumably knowing that they could not dispute his claim (1 Corinthians 14:18), Paul is able to chide them by remarking:

> Thank God, I speak in tongues more than
> any of you.

Who should pray?

As far as Paul is concerned, prayer is something that all his Christians should do. It is to be an activity of the whole Church, as he indicates in his first surviving letter (1 Thessalonians 5:25):

> Brothers and sisters, pray for us.

Or in 2 Thessalonians 3:1 (which admittedly may not be by Paul, but is typical of his style) we read:

> For the rest, pray for us, brothers and sisters,
> that the word of the Lord may run fluently.

NOT THAT MAN!

Prayer is not the preserve of a special 'praying class'. Widows, for example, are urged to pray:

> The one who is a genuine widow and really on her own has put her hope in God, and persists in supplication and prayer, night and day . . .
>
> *1 Timothy 5:5*

Paul assumes that not only Philemon, but all of the church who meet in his house will be praying for him:

> Make a guest-room ready for me at the same time, for I hope to be given to you all as a gift, through the prayers of all of you.
>
> *Philemon 22*

Paul absolutely depends on the Corinthians' prayers for him, even in a context where the relationship is on rocky ground:

> . . . with all of you also co-operating with your prayer for us . . .
>
> *2 Corinthians 1:11*

Epaphras is praying for the Colossians:

> Epaphras, who is one of you, a slave of Christ Jesus, sends you greetings. He is always doing battle in his prayers on your

> behalf; [he is praying] that you may stand
> perfect and fulfilled in every aspect of
> God's will.
> *Colossians 4:12*

There are many different ways of praying, but what matters is the effect on the group of Christians. When speaking to those divided Corinthians (1 Corinthians 14:26) Paul refers to it as 'building-up':

> Each of you has [something]: a psalm,
> a teaching, a revelation, a language,
> a translation. Let everything contribute to
> building-up . . .

What's the use of praying?

We do not quite know what it is we do when we pray but, in some way that we cannot quite pin down, it is a bridging of the gap between humanity and God, and the world is a better place for it. Of that, Paul is in no doubt whatever; here he is praying for the Thessalonians (2 Thessalonians 1:11–12), and he expects them to be praying for him (2 Thessalonians 3:1–2). The Roman church is also to pray for Paul:

> I am begging you, brothers and sisters,
> through our Lord Jesus Christ, and through
> the love of the Spirit, to do battle in your
> prayers to God on my behalf, that I may be
> delivered from the unbelievers in Judaea

> and that my collection for Jerusalem may
> become acceptable to the saints.
>
> *Romans 15:30–31*

Clearly, prayer is for Paul simply a part of the way in which the Christian groups express their role as actors in the age-old story of God. So it is not done in order to show off (see Matthew 6:5–8 for a comical account of how this might work out). Its function, as we have already seen, is to 'build-up'. This is how he works it out in that tricky 1 Corinthians 14. In verses 12–19, he writes:

> So you, since you are so keen on the spirits,
> be keen on the building-up of the church,
> that you may overflow. So – let the one
> who speaks in a tongue pray for the gift of
> translation; for if I pray in a tongue, my
> spirit prays, but my intellect is without fruit.
> What do you think? I'll pray in the spirit,
> but also in the intellect. I'll sing in the spirit,
> but also in the intellect. Because if you
> bless in the spirit, the person who takes the
> place of the outsider, how is that person
> going to utter the 'Amen' to your
> thanksgiving? Because he has no idea what
> you are saying. You give a good thanksgiving,
> but the other person is not built up. Thank
> God, I speak in tongues more than any of
> you – but I'd rather speak five words

with my intellect, in order to instruct other
people, than ten thousand words in a
tongue.

And the purpose of all this becomes clear later in the chapter (14:24–25):

If they're all prophesying, and an unbeliever
or an outsider comes in, they are shown up
by everybody, called to account by everybody, the secrets of their heart are laid
bare, they will fall on their face and worship
God, and announce, 'God really is with you
people!'

That is what it is all about. God is demonstrably in the church; the esteem in which individual Christians are held because of their prayer-life or striking manifestations of spirituality is entirely irrelevant.

Conclusion

In the end, what we may have to do is recognise, with Paul, that we simply do not know what we do when we pray, and that it does not matter, because we have to pray, even if we do not really understand what it is we are doing. Listen to this, one of his 'purple passages' as he draws to the close of his great account, in Romans 5–8, of why Christians can be confident:

> In just the same way, the Spirit assists our weakness; for we have no idea about praying as we ought to pray. No – but the Spirit himself pleads for us, in groans that can't be uttered. And the one who searches hearts knows what the Spirit is thinking, that in God's dispensation the Spirit is interceding for the saints.
>
> *Romans 8:26–27*

Do you think that prayer is important?
Does Paul have anything helpful to say about prayer?
Paul speaks of 'groans that can't be uttered'. What do you think he has in mind?

Seven
Paul on preaching

Francis of Assisi is said to have had the motto, 'Preach all the time; use words if you must.' And in the city where I live there is a person who regularly stands in one of the pedestrian thoroughfares, threatening passers-by with the most terrible sanctions if they do not repent and turn to Jesus. One is torn between admiration for his courage, and a mild resentment that he gives ammunition to those in the city who regard all Christians as lunatics.

It is something that Paul has to do, because he loves Jesus

For Paul, preaching is at the heart of who he is. In the following passage, he is talking about apostles' rights, and making it clear that above all he has to preach, or 'gospel':

> If I preach the gospel, there is nothing for me to boast about; you see, I am under a compulsion to do it. If I don't preach the gospel, I'm in trouble! If I do it of my own volition, I have my reward; if I do it despite myself, I have been entrusted with a commission. What is my reward? It is that in my 'gospelling', I should present the gospel at no charge, so as not to abuse my authority in the gospel.

> You see, although I am free in every respect, I made myself everyone's slave, in order to win over more people. And to the Jews I became like a Jew, in order to win over the Jews, to those under the Law [I became] like one under the Law, even though I was not myself under the Law, in order to win over those under the Law. To those who were Lawless I became like one who was Lawless; I wasn't Lawless as to the Law of God, but I was under the 'Law' of Christ, in order to win over the Lawless. I became weak for the weak, in order to win over the weak. I became all things to everybody, in order that in every way I might save some people. I do everything because of the gospel, in order to be in solidarity with the gospel.
>
> *1 Corinthians 9:16–23*

This is far from easy to translate, although the gist is clear; the only thing that matters to Paul is getting the message across; and he is quite willing to adopt any disguise as long as it preaches the gospel. Paul expresses the urgency of the matter in Romans 10: 14–17, in the middle of his wrestling with the problem of where his fellow Jews belong in God's story:

> So how will they call upon the name of one in whom they have not come to faith?

> And how will they come to faith in the one
> of whom they have not heard? And how
> will they hear unless there is a preacher?
> And how is someone to preach, unless they
> are sent? As it is written, *'How beautiful are
> the feet of those who gospel good things!'*
> The trouble is, not everyone has obeyed
> the gospel, for Isaiah says, *'Lord, who has
> believed what we have heard?'* So faith
> comes from hearing, and hearing comes
> from Christ's word . . .

There is a real urgency here, the same as drove Paul on his relentless pilgrimage round the cities of the Mediterranean. What matters above all is that his beloved Jesus should be proclaimed throughout the world, not only to Gentiles, but also to Paul's fellow Jews. This is what he is referring to as he starts to share his travel-plans with the Roman church:

> So I have [grounds for] boasting in Christ
> Jesus, with regard to the story of God.
> For I would not have the nerve to talk of
> anything except what Christ has
> accomplished through me, to bring the
> non-Jews into obedience in deed and word,
> with the power of signs and wonders,
> with the power of the Spirit of God.
> The upshot is that, starting from Jerusalem,
> and in a circle round as far as Illyricum,

> I have fulfilled Christ's gospel,
> considering it an honour to gospel
> where Christ has not been named,
> in order to avoid building on
> someone else's foundation . . .
>
> *Romans 15:17–20*

For our purposes, the point here is that once more Paul feels obliged to preach the gospel, and to bring it to where it has not been before. That is his mission:

> Christ did not send me to baptise, but to preach the gospel.
>
> *1 Corinthians 1:17*

Although he slightly spoils the effect by forgetting, and having to be reminded, in verses 15–16, that he did in fact baptise Crispus and Gaius, and the house of Stephanas. For Paul it is worth paying any price in order to do this preaching. He reminds the Thessalonians what it was like when he first came to them:

> Brothers and sisters, you yourselves know
> about our coming to you, and that it was
> not pointless. On the contrary, as you know,
> we had already suffered and been insulted
> at Philippi; but we still had the courage in
> our God to speak God's gospel, with much
> opposition.
>
> *1 Thessalonians 2:1–2*

Indeed, later in the same chapter (9–12) he indicates that preaching the gospel is the only thing that matters:

> ... for you remember, brothers and sisters, our labour and our toil; working night and day so as not to put a burden on any of you, we preached the gospel of God to you. You and God are our witnesses to the holiness and righteousness and blamelessness with which we approached you believers, just as you are aware how, like a father with his children, we treated each one of you, consoling and comforting you, and bearing witness to you, for each one of you to behave worthily of the God who calls you into his glorious Kingdom.

In 1 Timothy 2:7, the author, who may not be Paul although the sentiment is entirely plausible on Paul's lips, writes:

> ... for this I was set aside as a herald and an apostle (I am telling the truth, not lying), a teacher of the Gentiles in faith and in truth.

'This is what I do', might sum up his message here.

It matters what you preach: there is only one gospel

However not just any gospel will do. Paul is furious because the Galatians appear to have abandoned the gospel that he had given them:

> I am astonished that you have so quickly
> transferred from the one who called you in
> grace, to another gospel. But there is no
> other gospel! Apart from the people who
> are disturbing you and looking to pervert
> Christ's gospel. No – even if we or an angel
> from heaven were to gospel you differently
> from the gospel that we gospelled you, let
> them be accursed!
>
> *Galatians 1:6–8*

Three verses later (11–12), he is reminding them of the salient fact, that it is the gospel of God:

> I'm telling you, brothers and sisters, the
> gospel that was gospelled by me is not a
> human construct. I did not receive it from
> any human being, nor was I taught it.
> No – [it was] through a revelation of
> Jesus Christ.

The Colossians, whose problem is not easy to reconstruct with any confidence, are likewise warned not to shift from the original gospel:

> . . . if you remain founded and enthroned
> in the faith, and don't make any movement
> away from the hope that is the gospel that
> you heard, that which was preached in all
> creation under heaven, of which I Paul
> became a servant . . .
>
> *Colossians 1:23*

Paul clearly has strong views about what does and what does not count as the authentic gospel.

What is the content of this gospel?

It is worth asking ourselves what the gospel must contain. Firstly, it must be rooted in Scripture, and present itself as God's ancient story. So at Romans 1:16–17, Paul sums up his gospel in the following terms:

> You see, I am not embarrassed by the gospel; for it is God's power, for salvation to everyone who believes, first Jews and then Gentiles. For God's righteousness is revealed in it, from faith to faith, as it is written, 'The just person shall live out of faith'.

Paul ends this little summary with the quotation from Habakkuk 2:4 which is so important to the argument in Romans. In this letter, he is trying diplomatically to defend the gospel that he had earlier outlined in Galatians, rather more testily, that it is all a matter of God's free gift, and nothing at all to do with human merits; but humans have to respond by trusting God in Christ. And the name of that trust is 'faith'; and that means that anyone, whether born into Judaism or not, is able to belong in God's story.

Secondly, the gospel is all about Christ. You could almost stick a pin in the Pauline corpus to demonstrate this point, but consider the following texts. Paul is accused of being fickle; at the end of 1 Corinthians he said that he was hoping to visit that over-sensitive group of Christians, but by the time 2 Corinthians begins he has still not arrived; and so he writes:

> For the Son of God, Jesus Christ, the one
> who was preached among you through [us],
> was not 'Yes' and 'No'. On the contrary
> 'Yes' happened in him.
>
> *2 Corinthians 1:19*

It is Christ, and nothing else, that counts in preaching the gospel. It is certainly not Paul (4:5):

> ... for we do not proclaim ourselves, but
> Jesus Christ as Lord, and ourselves as your
> slaves because of Jesus.

It could not be clearer. Perhaps Paul's most touching expression of the absolute centrality of Christ is in Philippians 1:15–20, where he relates his prison experience, and the fact that (rather oddly, we may think):

> some people have been preaching Christ
> out of 'envy and factionalism', while some
> do it out of good will. Some do it out of
> love, knowing that I am in my present
> position as a way to defend the gospel;
> while others proclaim Christ out of selfish

ambition, insincerely, thinking that they will
arouse trouble for me in my imprisonment.
So what? [All that matters is that] in every
way, whether with false motives or true,
Christ is proclaimed – and I am rejoicing
at that.

Yes – and I shall rejoice, for I know that
this will turn out for my salvation, through
your entreaty and the generous gift of the
Spirit of Jesus Christ, according to my
eager expectation and hope, because I am
not going to be put to shame, but in all
confidence, as always, so today, Christ will
be glorified in my body, whether through
my life or through my death.

This is a heart-warming passage, filled with Paul's confidence and joy, and above all his passionate desire that Christ should be widely known.

Thirdly, and inevitably with Paul, it is all about the Resurrection. Wrestling with the difficult question of how the Jews fit into God's story (Romans 9–11), he makes this characteristic remark:

If you confess with your mouth that the
Lord is Jesus, and if you believe with your
heart that God raised him from the dead,
you will be saved.
Romans 10:9

Here Paul combines his faith in the Resurrection with his insistence on the lordship of Jesus. This is how Paul does his preaching, and underlines the urgency of the task.

It may be worth reminding you of the passage that we have already quoted, where he deals with the Corinthians' sceptical views about the Resurrection:

> I want you to know, brothers and sisters,
> the gospel that I gospelled to you, which
> you received, on which you have taken your
> stand, through which you are being saved,
> in what terms I gospelled to you, if you are
> holding it fast, unless you believed in vain.
>
> You see, I passed on to you in the first
> place, what I also received, that Christ
> **died** for our sins, in accordance with the
> Scriptures, and that he was **buried**,
> and that he was **raised** on the third day,
> in accordance with the Scriptures, and that
> he was **seen** . . .
>
> Now if Christ is being proclaimed
> among you as having been raised from the
> dead, how is it that some people among
> you are saying that there is no such thing as
> Resurrection from the dead?
>
> *1 Corinthians 15:1–5, 12*

The verbs in bold type are the heart of Paul's preaching (the 'gospel of four verbs'). There really was a Resurrection; Jesus was indeed dead, and his return from the dead was witnessed by those who knew him well. That was the model that Luke used in constructing Paul's sermon on the Areopagus (Acts 17:32). The Athenians simply roared with laughter, because resurrection, as every educated person is well aware, simply does not happen. Paul insists on preaching the Resurrection. That must be the model for preachers today. Would-be preachers might be helped by reflecting on the words of 2 Timothy 4:1–5 (whether written by Paul himself, or by a later disciple offering us 'what Paul would be saying today'), and allowing the words to challenge and encourage them:

> I adjure you, before God and before Christ Jesus, who is going to come to judge the living and the dead, and by his Manifestation and by his kingdom: proclaim the word; be ready, whether it is convenient or inconvenient; admonish, rebuke, console, in all patience and teaching.
>
> For a time will come when they will not put up with healthy teaching; instead, they will pile up teachers for themselves, titillating their ears, and turning their ears away from the truth, while directing them towards fables. But you must stay sober in every respect, bear hardship patiently, do the job of an evangelist, fulfil your service.

What is a preacher aiming to do?

For Paul, there is no question; he must, first, address the real problems of his people. So, in 1 Corinthians, for example, although the Corinthians have sent him a (possibly rather complacent) letter, he does not answer their questions, which presumably as far as Paul is concerned are not the real issues, until chapter 7. Instead he starts with what he thinks has really gone wrong:

> I'm begging you, brothers and sisters, through the name of Our Lord Jesus Christ, that you all say the same thing, and that there be no divisions among you, but that you be made complete in the same mind and the same opinion. You see, it has been revealed to me, brothers and sisters, by Chloe's people, that there are quarrels among you . . . !
> *1 Corinthians 1:10–11*

Having faced that, he must then think on his feet, and provide solutions that will work in that particular situation and at this particular time. Quite a good example of this thinking on his feet comes at the beginning of chapter 3 of the same letter, when he addresses both the particular and the general causes of the divisions:

> And as for me, brothers and sisters, I was unable to speak to you as spiritual people; no – I had to speak to you as fleshy people,

> as infants in Christ. I gave you milk to
> drink, not food; because you weren't yet up
> to it! And you're still not up to it; because
> you're still fleshy. You see, when there is
> jealousy and quarrelling among you, aren't
> you being fleshy, and behaving like [mere]
> human beings? You see, when someone
> says 'I'm for Paul', and someone else says,
> 'I'm for Apollos', aren't you being [just]
> human?
>
> *1 Corinthians 3:1–4*

Then Paul spends the rest of the chapter offering two analogies, from building and from gardening, to illuminate the roles that he and Apollos play in the church, and to demonstrate that factionalism comes from a lack of attention to what is really going on, that God is in charge here, and not the different possible leaders within the Church.

Secondly, the preacher should never be afraid to challenge his people. So at Romans 2:1, just as he has lulled the Jewish members of the Roman church into complacently nodding 'Yes, Paul, give it to them hot and strong,' as he lists the ways in which the Gentiles get it wrong, he turns on them too and imperiously lectures them:

> So you, that is any human being who
> condemns, have no defence . . .

Or consider 1 Corinthians 5:1:

> It is even said that there is sexual
> immorality among you, and sexual
> immorality even of a kind that you don't
> find among Gentiles, in that a man has his
> father's wife!

or 6:1:

> One of you has the nerve, when you have
> a disagreement, to go to law against a fellow
> Christian, in the courts of the unjust, and
> not of the saints!

The Corinthians are still impatiently waiting for him to answer their letter, but instead he challenges them about incest in the group and about their litigious activity. Or at 2 Corinthians 8:1–2 he starts a long attempt to persuade that rather wealthy church to get their hands out of their pockets and contribute generously to their impoverished fellow Christians in Jerusalem:

> We are letting you know, brothers and
> sisters, about the generosity for God given
> by the churches of Macedonia; in the midst
> of a great ordeal of affliction, the overflow
> of their joy and their deep poverty
> overflowed into the wealth of their
> liberality . . .

Very quietly, Paul challenges the Corinthians by offering them an alternative example, from a church that really did not have much in the way of financial solidity.

On the other hand, a preacher should never become so determined to challenge the complacent that his (or her) people are left without hope. Paul is the apostle of the Resurrection, the best possible grounds for hope, and always reminds them (even the Galatians and the Corinthians) that the horrors of our present existence are not the end of the story. Here is a line to the Romans that may stand for the rest:

> For I reckon that the sufferings of our
> present moment are not fit to be
> considered in comparison with the glory
> that is about to be revealed to us . . .
>
> *Romans 8:18*

Challenging and condemning iniquity is great fun, and makes a preacher feel enormously superior to the unfortunates who are being harangued; but it is not in the end constructive, if all preaching is negative.

What methods of preaching should one employ?

Occasionally one hears of preachers who are technologically masterful, who can entrance their congregations with glittering displays of video and audio material. Repressing a spurt of unworthy envy for their omnicompetence, we may nevertheless reflect, with Paul, that clever tricks are not all that important:

> ... [when I came to you] my rhetoric and my preaching were not in the honeyed terms of spin-doctoring, but in the demonstration of the Spirit's power, so that your faith should depend, not on clever human tricks, but on the power of God ... the things that we speak of, not in the learned rhetoric of human cleverness, but in the 'rhetoric' that is taught by the Spirit, interpreting spiritual things to spiritual people.
>
> *1 Corinthians 2:4–5, 13*

Nor (as some of us agree with relief) do you have to be a brilliant preacher. There were those at Corinth who were rather critical of Paul's techniques, it seems:

> Look at what is before your eyes!
> If someone is self-confident enough
> to regard themselves as belonging to Christ,
> so do we. You see, if it is permissible for me
> to boast a little more fully about our
> mission, which the Lord gave us (to build
> you up, not to destroy you), I'm not going
> to be embarrassed, thinking about how I
> might terrorise you with my letters.
> They say, 'His letters are impressive and
> powerful; but his physical presence is

> unimpressive, and as for his *rhetoric* . . .!'
> People like this should reflect that we are
> just the same in our rhetoric in absentia in
> our letters as we are when we are present
> with you for real! . . . you see, it's not the
> person who commends themselves who is
> tried and tested; no – it's the one whom the
> Lord recommends.
>
> *2 Corinthians 10:7–18*

Paul is clearly quite cross here, not just because he has been unfavourably compared with more brilliant spin-doctors, but because his wretched Corinthians do not properly understand what is going on.

The fact is, what is important in preaching is simply this: to get across what really matters. And what is that? Ask Paul, and hear what he says:

> Since, while Jews are asking for signs,
> and Gentiles are looking for cleverness, we,
> on the other hand, preach Christ crucified,
> a scandal for Jews, and sheer stupidity
> for Gentiles; but to those who are called,
> both Jews and Gentiles, Christ the power of
> God and God's 'cleverness' . . .
>
> *1 Corinthians 1:22–24*

Here we should simply listen to Paul telling us 'where it's at', in this matter of preaching.
What is the importance of preaching?
Does Paul offer any help to would-be preachers?

Eight

Paul on Church leadership

It may surprise some readers to learn this, but Paul was not a priest. He is often depicted as such (indeed some pictures of him include a bishop's mitre) and, as we shall see, there is at least one occasion when Acts seems to present him in a priestly function. At least once, he uses priestly language to describe his work:

> I am writing to you a bit more audaciously, reminding you of the grace given to me by God, so that I am a minister *(leitourgos – the word is connected with 'liturgy')* of Christ Jesus to the Gentiles, serving the gospel of God like a priest, so that the Gentiles' Offertory may be acceptable, consecrated in the Holy Spirit.
> *Romans 15:15–16*

Here one suspects that Paul is deliberately using such language, not because he regards himself as a priest, but because this kind of talk would mean something to the Jewish Christians in his audience in Rome, who may have been a bit suspicious of him. Nevertheless, it is interesting that he describes his work in terms of language drawn from the Jewish temple worship.

On one occasion, described by Luke in Acts 20, Paul serves as a stern warning against garrulous preaching:

> On one of the Sabbaths *(or: the first day of the week)*, when we had gathered to break bread, Paul was talking to them, because he was due to go away the following day. And he extended his sermon until the middle of the night. There were a good many lamps in the upper room where we had gathered. And a certain young man called Eutychus was sitting on the windowsill, and sinking into a deep sleep, as Paul went on and on; overwhelmed by sleep, he fell down from the third storey, and was taken up dead! Paul went down and threw himself upon him, and embracing him said, 'Don't be disturbed, because his soul *(or: his life)* is still in him.' He came up and broke bread, and having tasted a fair amount, he preached *(or: conversed)* until dawn. And so he left. And they took the child alive, and they were very greatly comforted.
>
> *Acts 20:7–12*

It is not precisely clear what is going on here, but Paul does not seem to have learnt the lesson from the effect on Eutychus, since having talked first until midnight, he then carried on until dawn! If this was a Christian Eucharist, it is not obvious that Paul was what nowadays we should call the 'president' or 'celebrant'.

Was Paul a 'pastor', then? Not surprisingly, the image occurs quite frequently on Jesus' lips (John 10:11; Luke 15:1–7; Matthew 18:12–14; 25:31–46), but of course Jesus was a 'country boy', for whom such pictures were part of where he came from. The idea is common enough in the Jewish scriptures, which fed both Jesus and Paul, but despite that Paul only twice uses the image of 'pastor' or 'shepherd', so far as I can see. The first is at 1 Corinthians 9:7, where it is part of an argument to the effect that Christian apostles have certain rights (though Paul has elected not to make use of those rights). The other use of the word 'shepherds' is in Ephesians 4:11 (which may not have been written by Paul, of course), where it is one of a list of functionaries within the body of Christ. Here it is sandwiched between 'evangelists' and 'teachers'.

What is Christian leadership not about?

No matter how tempting the idea may be for Christian leaders, ministry in the church is not a matter of gaining popularity. Paul spends most of 1 Corinthians clarifying the respective functions of himself and Apollos; for it looks as though the parties gathered round those two were the fault lines on which that church was divided. He concludes:

> So let a person regard us as servants of Christ, and stewards of God's mysteries. So in this connection, what is required of stewards is that they should turn out as reliable *(or: faithful)*. It is of no importance to me that I should be submitted to a judicial hearing by you, or by any human court.
>
> *1 Corinthians 4:1–3*

Here, Paul is not trying to win friends among the Corinthians, but to make it clear to them that they have no particular rights over him. This does not mean that Paul is unaccountable, however (the great temptation of Christian ministry); he will have to answer to God, and to Christ. So in verse 4 he says 'it is the Lord who calls me to account'. He is not particularly interested in winning the Corinthians' esteem.

Nor, for Paul, is Christian leadership about winning a popularity contest. In a rage, he turns on the Galatians, and addresses them as 'you **stupid** Galatians', or, as a colleague has suggested, 'you crazy Celts'. He is quite capable of using sarcasm, as in this passage:

> You are already filled up! You have already attained wealth! With no help from us, you have become kings! I wish that you *had* become kings, so that we might be kings with you! You see, I think that God has revealed us apostles as last [of all], as condemned to death, because we have become a laughing stock for the world, and for angels, and for human beings . . .
> *1 Corinthians 4:8–9*

Or look at this passage, to the same Corinthians, when they had allowed themselves to think that perhaps Paul was not a *real* apostle (2 Corinthians 11:19–20):

> For you gladly put up with fools, being so clever yourselves. You'd put up with it if

people were to sell you into slavery, or if
they were to gobble you up, or capture you,
or put on airs, or slap you in the face!

And on one occasion (1 Corinthians 4:21), Paul even threatens them with corporal punishment, and the Corinthians may have been uncertain whether he meant it, even though he is here defending his more gentle approach:

What do you want? Do you want me to
come at you with a stick? Or in love and a
spirit of meekness?

Nor, on the other hand, does Christian ministry have anything to do with making money, as far as Paul is concerned. Oddly enough, they have been attacking him in Corinth because he did not take their money (this is not currently a regular accusation against church leaders). So we hear him insisting on his rights, in 1 Corinthians 9:3–12:

My defence against those who are putting
me on trial is this: Don't we also have the
right to eat and drink? Don't we have the
right to take a Christian wife around with us,
just like the rest of the apostles, and the
brothers of the Lord, and Kephas? Or is it
just Barnabas and I who don't have the
right not to work?

There follow three examples, from military service, from farming, and from looking after sheep, after which Paul asserts:

> But we did not make use of this right;
> no – we put up with everything,
> in order not to put any obstacle
> in the way of Christ's gospel.

What then does Paul get out of it? If we can believe him, and you would have to be very brave to contest the matter with him, his reward is nothing else than to preach the gospel:

> So – what's my reward? It is that I should
> present the gospel free of charge, so as not
> to make use of my gospel authority. You
> see, although I was free in every respect,
> I made myself a slave to everybody, in
> order to win over a few more.
>
> *1 Corinthians 9:18–19*

In the second letter to those Corinthians, he gets quite cross, not to say sarcastic, on this issue:

> Or did I commit a sin, in abasing myself so
> that you might be exalted, when I gospelled
> the gospel of God to you at no charge?
> I robbed other churches, when I accepted
> support from them in order to serve you.
>
> *2 Corinthians 11:7–8*

It is a matter of immense importance to him that he made no money out of his preaching. In the first of his extant letters, he reminds the Thessalonians:

> [Surely you remember] my labour and toil
> for you, brothers and sisters, working night
> and day so as not to oppress any of you
> when we proclaimed God's gospel to you.
>
> *1 Thessalonians 2:9*

One thing that Paul is clear about, something that the people of our day perhaps need to hear, is that there is real freedom in working for nothing. It is degrading and dispiriting, of course, to be exploited; but there is nothing dehumanising about willingly surrendering oneself to the providence of God.

What is Christian leadership about?

In the first place, it is about affection. Paul is genuinely fond even of his Galatians and Corinthians. So we hear him tell the latter:

> I'm not writing these things to you to
> shame you, but to warn you, as my beloved
> children. For you may have had ten
> thousand disciplinarians in Christ, but not
> many fathers; for in Christ Jesus, through
> the gospel, it was **I** that brought you to birth.
>
> *1 Corinthians 4:14–15*

Here Paul speaks lovingly of his fellow Jews:

> I'm telling the truth in Christ; I'm not lying;
> my conscience bears witness to me in the
> Holy Spirit, that it is a great grief to me, and
> an unceasing pain to my heart. For I made it
> my prayer that **I** should become *anathema*
> from Christ, for the sake of my fellow Jews ...
>
> *Romans 9:1–3*

This person loves passionately. Listen to him talking about the Philippians, perhaps his favourite group of Christians:

> I give thanks to my God whenever
> I remember you, always, in all my prayers
> for all of you, joyfully making my prayers,
> because of the gospel solidarity you showed,
> from the first day until the present ...
>
> *Philippians 1:3–5*

Paul is properly described as 'a great lover'; indeed he so describes himself, in his first extant epistle:

> ... as a mother suckles her own children,
> so we longed for you, and were pleased to
> give over to you, not only the gospel of
> God, but also our own lives, because you
> had become beloved to us ...
>
> *1 Thessalonians 2:7–8*

In the next chapter (3:9–10) he continues the theme:

> ... for what thanksgiving can we return to
> the Lord for you, in all the joy with which
> we rejoice before our God, day and night
> begging most earnestly to see your face,
> and to make good what is lacking in your
> faith?

And Paul's affection includes those whom his correspondents might otherwise disdain, such as Phoebe (Romans 16:1), and Timothy, whom he was evidently afraid that the Corinthians might disdain, on the grounds that they wanted 'the organ-grinder, not his monkey':

> And if Timothy comes, make sure that he
> does not have a fearful time with you; for
> he is doing the Lord's work just as I myself
> am. So no one is to disdain him. Send him
> on his way in peace, for him to come to me;
> for I am waiting for him, with the brothers
> and sisters ...   *1 Corinthians 16:10–11*

(You will surely be correct in reading a certain menace in that last phrase). Or read for yourself Philippians 2:25–30, and see the gentle affection for Epaphroditus in those verses.

In addition to affection as a quality of Christian leadership, Paul also follows his master in asserting the importance of service (see, for example, Mark 10:45). So when Paul is trying to sort out the little local difficulty over himself and Apollos, he makes this important statement, that Christian leaders will do well to remember:

> So what is Apollos? What is Paul? [They are] **servants**, through whom you came to faith ...
>
> *1 Corinthians 3:5*

(Compare this with 2 Corinthians 3:6; 11:23). This instinct, to serve rather than dominate (though one is forced to admit that Paul would not always be innocent of any desire for domination!), has quite practical consequences, as we see when he is making arrangements for the collection for the saints in Jerusalem with his mistrustful Corinthians:

> ... when I come, the people whom you approve, I shall send off with letters, to carry your gift to Jerusalem. And if it is appropriate for me to make the journey also, they will journey with me.
>
> *1 Corinthians 16:3–4*

Paul here recognises, important though the collection is to him, that he may have to hold back, and respect the choices of the Corinthians who seem to have lost confidence in him. This is a profound act of service.

More generally, Christian leadership for Paul is a matter of acting on a few basic principles, and then working out the answers to problems as they arise. His basic principles would be that God raised Jesus from the dead, that Jesus is Lord, that God is faithful, and that Paul's mission is to the Gentiles, and that, to solve all problems, above all it is necessary to keep our eyes on Jesus. If you combine Philippians 4:2, when he tells Evodia and Syntyche to have 'the same mindset in the Lord', with 2:1–11, where Paul exhorts the wider Philippian church to have the same mindset as Jesus, you will see how Paul's approach to any problem is to get people to keep their eyes on Jesus. Paul is a pastoral rather than an academic theologian, and it is in that context that Paul has the nerve to encourage his Corinthians (1 Corinthians 4:1; 11:1) and Thessalonians (1 Thessalonians 1:6) to imitate him; this is not arrogance, I think, but an attempt to do what Jesus would do, including enduring the suffering that will inevitably come with Christian leadership.

More than anything else, Christian leadership is about preaching. This does not necessarily mean standing on a soap box, or at a street corner, or even in a pulpit, so much as making known the basic principles about Christ, by every means available.

Christian leadership and the Eucharist

Certainly, for Paul, Christian leadership has something to do with the Eucharist; but we must be careful here. Questions about who may preside at the Eucharist had not yet made their appearance, and indeed one suspects Paul might have looked askance at the hidden power games underlying those questions. For him the relationship between Christian leadership and the Eucharist came in three ways.

First, the Eucharist has Christ at its centre, and not anyone else. When he is trying to sort out a difficult question about eating food that has been offered to idols, Paul approaches it from this angle (1 Corinthians 10:16–17), and insists on the unity that it brings:

> The cup of blessing which we bless, is it
> not a solidarity with the blood of Christ?
> The bread which we break, is it not a
> solidarity with the body of Christ? Because
> we who are many are one loaf, one body, for
> all of us have shared from the same loaf.

Second, and following on from this, Paul asserts the equality of all Christians in a Eucharistic context. Here the target is those Christians who are class-conscious, and who make distinctions between their fellow Christians:

> . . . when you come together, it is not for
> better, but for worse. For in the first place,
> when you come together as a church, I hear
> that there are divisions among you! And in
> part I believe it. Because there need to be
> factions among you, so that the tried and
> tested can be revealed among you.
>   So, when you come together, **it is not to**

> **eat the Lord's Supper!** For each one takes his or her own supper when they eat, and one goes hungry, while another is drunk! Don't you have homes for eating and drinking in? Do you despise the Church of God, and put the have-nots to shame?
>
> *1 Corinthians 11:17–22*

Having delivered himself of this broadside, Paul then proceeds to indicate what Jesus did (and, once again, we are grateful for him getting cross, because of what it makes him reveal):

> For I received from the Lord, what I also handed down to you, that the Lord Jesus, on the night on which he was being betrayed, took bread, and when he had given thanks, broke it, and said, 'This is my body, which is for you. Do this for my memory.' Likewise the cup, after supper, saying, 'This cup is the new covenant in my blood. Do this, as often as you drink it, for my memory.' For as often as you eat this bread and drink this cup, you are proclaiming the death of the Lord, until he comes.
>
> *1 Corinthians 11:23–26*

Because of what Jesus did, all Christians are equal at the Eucharist.

Third, all Christians are interdependent at the Eucharist. Paul expresses this with his analogy of the body (1 Corinthians 12:4–31) which he outlines with humour and originality and deft application to the Corinthian situation, and then brings to a wonderful climax in the great hymn to love that is 1 Corinthians 13.

If all this is so, then Christian leadership is to be exercised in a restrained and utterly unselfish way; all Christians depend upon each other, all are equal, and all are to be centred on Christ and him alone.

Is 'leadership' needed in the Christian Church?
Does Paul have anything helpful to say about how such leadership might work?

Nine

Paul and the outside world

Introduction

Whatever country you are living in, wherever you are reading or hearing these words, each will have its own particular set of problems; and for Christians it is always essential that they are alert to the problems and the cultural presuppositions that are operative in that society. All societies have their difficulties, but all have their good points, and Christians cannot cut themselves off from the 'outside world'. So it may be a good idea, before you start this chapter, to identify the biggest problems facing 'this' country today, and the solutions you think should be adopted.

Paul and his Corinthians, indeed the communities of all the churches to which he wrote, had to live in the real world. The community of Christians in Corinth cannot have been more than 300 at the very outside. This is a tiny group, given that the population of Corinth will have been something like 30,000 (to judge by the amount of cultivable land available in the area). So we do not have to think of Paul as known to absolutely everybody in Corinth. Nevertheless, he is quite clear that his Christians do need to interact with outsiders (1 Corinthians 5:10).

The question may however arise for Christians what their attitude should be to the government of their time and place; and in many situations, the answer might be far from obvious. Sixteenth-century Catholics in England, Scotland and Wales found themselves obliged by law to deny their faith and to cease practising it. Some went along with government policy, with mental reservations, while others simply refused, at great personal cost. In South Africa, likewise, in the days of apartheid, some Christians reluctantly went along with government policy, while others resisted and ended up dead or in prison or solitary confinement. Others again, sadly, thought that Christianity and apartheid were compatible, and argued that anything was better than being communist. It will not invariably be obvious which way a Christian should go in a particular political situation.

The subversive claim: Jesus is Lord

The non-negotiable fact for Paul is the lordship of Jesus. 'Of course,' you say, 'we knew that.' But consider: if Jesus is Lord, then the emperor is not, and to be a Christian means that the state can never have absolute claims on us. That is true where you live today quite as much as it was in Paul's day. And it will mean trouble. There were more Christian martyrs in the twentieth century than in all the nineteen previous centuries put together, so it is certainly possible that as a Christian you will one day find yourself up against the claims of the state. The legend is that both Paul and Peter died, separately, but at the hands of a Roman emperor anxious to distract people's attention from allegations that he was responsible for the great fire of Rome in AD 64. The emperor's name, of course, was Nero, who may have been the first holder of that office actually to hear of 'Christians' as a recognisable group.

So it is that we find Paul in prison writing the letter to the Philippians, which some scholars place quite late in his career. Listen to how he writes:

> Christ is being proclaimed, and that makes me rejoice, for I know that in the end that will mean salvation for me, through your prayers, and through the generosity of the Spirit of Jesus Christ, in accordance with my eager expectation and hope, that I shall not be put to shame in any way; but in all openness, as always, and still today, Christ is going to be glorified in my body, whether through [my] life or through [my] death.
>
> For to me, Christ is life, and death is sheer profit. If I die in the flesh, that is gain from my work. And I have no idea which I shall choose; I am torn between the two, for I have a longing to dissolve and be with Christ (for that is much better); but to remain in the flesh is more necessary on your account.
>
> *Philippians 1:18b–24*

Paul is in prison at the behest of the emperor who wants to be called 'Lord', and the chances are that he will not come out alive (on the whole you did not emerge alive from ancient prisons), but he really does not mention Nero at all. Paul's only concern is with Christ, the object of his love, and the Philippians, who are his brothers and sisters in Christ. The imperial claims to lordship, a key element of the culture in which he lived, simply do not interest Paul.

Paul demonstrates the same calm indifference to the suffering that comes from his affirmation of Jesus' lordship over the dominant secular culture, when he writes to the Corinthians, in the context of proclaiming:

> Jesus as Lord, and ourselves as your slaves on Jesus' account . . . we have this treasure in clay vessels . . . oppressed in every respect, but not cramped, scratching our heads, but not foxed, hassled, but never abandoned, cast down but not destroyed, always carrying around Jesus' putting-to-death in our body, so that Jesus' life might be made clear in our body. For all the time we who are alive are being handed over to death, in order that Jesus' life might be made clear in our mortal flesh. So death is at work in us, but life in you.
>
> *2 Corinthians 4:5; 7–12*

Paul is quite calm, but clear-eyed, about the implications of asserting the lordship of Jesus; the dominant culture will react badly to that, and persecution is in consequence only to be expected. It may be helpful to remember that the Greek word for 'church' (*ekklesia*) has to do with being 'called-out' of the world.

But you still have to live in the real world

Nevertheless, you cannot wish the dominant culture away. It is there and, for most of the time, you have to live with it. This may explain why in Romans we find the passage we shall be dealing with next. This passage (Romans 13:1–8) caused great difficulties in South Africa in the apartheid days, because various church leaders were summoned to the office of the then president, who then read it to them, and told them that it was God's wish that they should obey him:

> Let everybody be subordinated to the
> governing authorities. You see, there is no
> authority that does not come from God,
> and the authorities that exist are ordered by
> God. So any who resist the authority have
> set themselves up against God's ordinance.
> And those who set themselves up in
> opposition will bring judgement on
> themselves. For those who rule are not
> scary for good deeds, but for bad deeds.
> Do you want to avoid being scared of
> authority? [Then] do good, and you
> will have praise from them. For the
> authority is God's servant, for you,
> to bring [you] benefits.

> But if you do what is bad, then be scared; for it is no accident that they carry weapons. For they are God's servant, an avenger to bring [God's] anger on those who do evil. Therefore, it is necessary to be subordinated, [and] not just because of [God's] anger, but also because of conscience.
>
> You see, that's the reason for paying taxes, because they are servants of God busy about that very purpose. So give everyone what you owe; if you owe someone tribute, pay them the tribute; if you owe someone tolls, pay them tolls. If you owe someone reverence, then give them reverence; if you owe someone honour, give them honour. Owe nothing to anybody, except to love each other. For the person who loves has fulfilled the rest of the Law . . .

What is going on here? Certainly, we should have to say that the Elder John who wrote the Book of Revelation would be shifting uneasily at this, for he had no time for the Roman authorities, and regarded them as the Antichrist. There are various comments that we might appropriately make.

In the first place, Paul had never heard of South Africa, and would in any case have been rather surprised to think of a South African president reading that passage to church leaders several centuries down the line. Secondly, we have to admit that we are in the dark here; it is not at all improbable that there was an issue in Rome about precisely this question of paying taxes. Some may have held that to pay taxes was in effect giving in to an immoral government, and implied worship of the emperor or of the pagan gods. Others may have responded that the Romans were not as bad as all that ('aqueducts, sanitation, roads, irrigation, medicine, education, wine, public baths and peace', as the Popular Front for the Liberation of Judaea grudgingly conceded in the film *The Life of Brian*). So it is possible that there was real tension in the Christian community in Rome, which had been largely Jewish Christian, and may by now have been largely Gentile. The Jewish element in the community will not have been immune to the anti-Roman stirrings in Palestinian Judaism that were to erupt in the first Jewish war, not long after Paul's death (AD 66–70).

Paul himself, as we have seen, seems to have been quite proud of being a Roman citizen, if Luke has him right; and certainly his apostolic work will have been greatly assisted by the excellent roads that the Romans built, all leading to Rome, as the saying goes, and by the postal service (better, some allege, than in the city of Rome today), and the fact that one could travel without fear of pirates across the Mediterranean. The preaching of the gospel is helped by the Roman infrastructure, and the communications and good order that it provides.

It is also possible that Paul has here made use of an existing Hellenistic treatise in favour of obedience to civil authorities; there is no Christology here, and a rather odd understanding of God, as well as absolutely no indication that the world is shortly coming to an end.

There is one further point: notice what he says at the end, 'Owe nothing to anybody, except to love each other. For the person who loves has fulfilled the rest of the Law . . .' If you take that seriously, then all the rest is relativised. Paul is here clearly alluding to the answer given by his beloved Jesus to the tricky question of the number one commandment (see Mark 12:28–34). Once you have said that, then nothing else matters, and the Romans may well have picked up the hidden message, that above all, and despite all their disagreements, the only thing that mattered was that they should love each other and the civil authorities as well. We might also notice that if the civil authorities are indeed 'ordered by God' and 'God's servant', then they are accountable to God. For our purpose in this chapter, it may be sufficient simply to observe that the relationship of Christians to secular political authority is never an easy one.

But the powers do not have authority over us

Nevertheless, in the end, Christians do not allow absolute claims to any other power than that of Jesus and God. This is how Paul, or one of his later interpreters, expresses it to a group that seems to have been anxious about those other powers:

> You were dead because of [your]
> transgressions, and because of the
> uncircumcision of your flesh, and he made
> you alive together with him, giving you a
> free pardon of all your transgressions,
> wiping out the bond, with its requirements,
> that stood against us, taking it out of the
> midst of us, and nailing it to the cross.
> He disarmed the principalities and powers,
> and made a public example of them,
> triumphing over them in it.
>
> *Colossians 2:13–15*

Here the 'powers' are partly political authorities, and partly supernatural enemies. The point is simple: that Jesus is powerful enough to cope with the mess that we are in, whatever form it may take, and that it is Jesus, and not the 'powers', that will be ultimately victorious.

Certainly the image that Paul uses at the end, 'He disarmed the principalities and powers ... triumphing' will have echoed for his readers one regular way in which the secular and imperial authorities demonstrated their muscle. If you win a victory over some faraway people, you are allowed to march through Rome with your legions. Normally, and for very sensible reasons, the legionary armies were not allowed near Rome; but if you had defeated a nation whom Rome had classed as an enemy, then you could have a victory parade through the city, showing the captives whom you had taken, and the booty that you had amassed. For an example of that, see Titus' Arch, recording the triumph of Titus, son of the Emperor Vespasian, after his conquest and destruction of Jerusalem.

The daring claim here, therefore, is that Jesus has triumphed over all the secular and spiritual powers, even 'nailing [them] to the cross'. We may imagine Paul's readers stirring at the thought.

Here is another passage that is germane to this issue:

> As it is, Christ is risen from the dead, the first-fruits of those who have fallen asleep. Because since Death [came] through a human being, it was also through a human being that the Resurrection from the dead [came]. For as in Adam all die, so also in Christ shall all be made alive, but each in their own proper order. Christ is the first-fruits, then those who belong to Christ, at his Coming. Then, at the end, when he hands the kingdom over to [his] God and Father, when he cancels out all rule and authority and power. For it is necessary for him to reign until he places all enemies under his feet. The last enemy to be cancelled out is Death, 'for he has

> subordinated all under his feet'. Now when it says, 'all is subordinated', clearly that does not include the one who subordinated everything to him. But when everything is subordinated to him, then the Son himself will be subordinated to the One who subordinated everything to him, in order that God might be all in all.
>
> *1 Corinthians 15:20–28*

This passage is a part of the penultimate chapter of 1 Corinthians, where Paul is speaking of the Resurrection of Christ; it talks, of course, of 'all rule and authority and power', which clearly refers to the secular political leaders. It also talks of that other power, which we must capitalise as 'Death', which Adam's transgression somehow let loose in the world. The point for us is that the ultimate sanction that the secular powers can impose is precisely Death; and if even that is not ultimately victorious, then our relationships with the 'secular city' can be entirely confident; we shall survive the worst that they can do. And notice, as always, how Paul locates his argument fully in the heart of the story of God and of Jesus, whose Coming will put all secular powers firmly in their place, and whose kingdom outweighs all possible human political arrangements.

Another passage that powerfully asserts that there are no powers, of whatever sort, that can seriously cause us to wobble is of course Romans 8:33–39, which we looked at earlier:

> Who will bring charges against God's chosen ones? It is God who justifies. Who brings in a verdict of 'Guilty'? Christ Jesus is the one who dies, but, more importantly, was raised, who is also at the right hand of God, who is also interceding for us. Who shall separate us from the love of Christ? Shall tribulation, or being-in-a-tight-place, or persecution, or not-having-anything-to-eat or having-nothing-to-wear, or danger, or lethal weapons? As it is written, 'For your sake, we are being put to death all day long. We are regarded as sheep for the abattoir.' But in all these things, we are winning a most glorious victory, through the One who loved us. For I am persuaded that neither Death, nor Life, nor angels nor rulers, nor things present nor things to come, nor powers, nor height nor depth, nor any other created thing, will be able to separate us from the love of God which is in Christ Jesus our Lord.

Once again, the solution to all the 'powers' that might menace us is found in the story of God and of Jesus, and their love for humanity. We can hardly follow Paul as he lists the various 'powers' that might separate us from that love, but we get the gist, which is that nothing is finally going to make that breach between us and God. In the end, even political powers, important and undeniably powerful as they are, do not exercise any absolute claim over us. Once more, the Resurrection, and Jesus' status in the story of God, is central to Paul's understanding of the present situation of Christians. And, as the Romans will have known, Paul could fairly claim to have experienced all the possible difficulties that might have separated him from Christ's love.

The fact is, although Christians have to 'live in the real world', they also look beyond it to a home that is with God. In Philippians, as we have said, Paul is in prison, perhaps in Rome, certainly in a setting governed by Rome's writ, for he speaks of the Praetorian Guard (1:14); and although he is happy to live in the Roman Empire, with all its advantages, it is not where, in the end, he belongs. So he writes to the Philippians exhorting them:

> Just exercise your citizenship in a way that
> is worthy of Christ's gospel . . . (1:27),

and later in the letter, with the conflicting claims of Roman citizenship and being 'in Christ' clearly very much on his mind, he tells them:

> . . . for we have a political existence [the
> Greek word here is *politeuma*] in heaven,
> from where we are expecting a Saviour, the
> Lord Jesus Christ; he is going to transform
> the body of our humiliation into the body

> of his glory, in accordance with the power
> that enables him to subordinate everything
> to him. So, my beloved and longed-for
> brothers and sisters, my joy and my crown,
> stand firm in the Lord in this way –
> beloved!
>
> *Philippians 3:20–4:1*

Here, Paul is clearly thinking of the conflicting claims of the body politic and the body of Christ: the word *politeuma* (which could mean, as we have translated above, 'political existence', 'commonwealth', 'state' or 'country') makes that clear; and so does his use of the word 'Saviour'. For Paul, the saviour had to be Jesus, but since the days of Augustus, Roman emperors had bestowed this title on themselves. Likewise, Paul's use of the word 'Lord' is no accident; it is Jesus and no emperor, who exercises dominion. They can, Paul is arguing, 'humiliate the body'; that is what is happening to Paul in prison. What they cannot do is what God did in the Resurrection: bring about a transformation into the 'body of glory'. Notice how once again the idea surfaces of 'subordinating everything to him'. We have already seen how Paul regards this as an essential part of what is going on in the Resurrection of Jesus. It is easy therefore to understand how Paul can be so extraordinarily joyful in this letter, written in such dire circumstances. The last line of the above passage simply radiates his joy and his passion for his fellow Christians, which neither suffering nor the possible imminence of death can thwart.

Conclusion: coping with the new ideology

Paul and probably all writers of the New Testament were writing against the background of an emerging ideology of empire. The old system of the Roman republic had collapsed, and Rome's reach now extended far beyond the city-state for which the republican system had evolved. It was simply no longer practicable to have two consuls who changed each year and had command of the legionary armies. It was virtually inevitable that the system of 'one man in charge' (for which the Latin was *princeps*), who would have *imperium* (control of the army) would evolve to deal with the change of status. The difficulty was that of succession. For the first half-century or so of the Empire it was handed down through the increasingly eccentric Julio-Claudian family; then, after Nero's suicide in AD 68, came the catastrophic 'year of the four emperors', from which Vespasian emerged victorious, leaving the sack of Jerusalem to his son Titus, and starting the Flavian dynasty that would take Rome to the end of the first century.

The old system had fallen apart (though it was not politically convenient to admit that fact) and the new was not in great shape. In addition, Paul and all our New Testament writers would have been brought up on the ancient Jewish critique of monarchy found in the prophets, not to mention Daniel and the Book of Wisdom and even the Dead Sea Scrolls. So when these Christians started employing, as part of the regular discourse of their faith, words that had track record in the Roman political dispensation, there was bound to be a clash. Such words included, of course, *Soter* (Saviour), and *Kyrios*, and *euangelion,* and *parousia* (which in the Roman political system referred to the arrival of an emperor or the like, but for Christians referred to Christ's second coming), or 'justification'. And when Christians like Paul proudly insisted on the fact of the Cross, a Roman punishment, tension with the establishment was inevitable. In favour of the Empire was the fact that God wants an orderly world; but emperors and their delegates had to realise their accountability to God, and if they started making absolute claims, then there was bound to be trouble.

It may be worth reflecting that a shrewd political analyst, observing these Christians in the mid-60s AD as they went to their deaths or were used as human torches to illuminate the guests at Nero's garden parties, would have seen that there was an inevitable and deep-seated tension between the Jesus-group and the vast Roman political machine; it is unlikely, however, that such an analyst would have been able to predict accurately which of the two groups was going to win.

Does Paul offer any help to you about how to live in the country where you find yourself today?
Should you be engaged with 'the powers that be?'

Ten
Paul and slavery

Christians often find themselves puzzling over their proper attitude to political institutions. Sometimes it takes the form of 'let us not get involved in politics – that's other people's business'; sometimes Christians feel a passionate call, arising out of their reading of the gospel, to reach out to the poor and marginalised, and to analyse the circumstances that make them so. In Paul's world, the institution of slavery took various forms, but it was part of the economic reality of the Roman empire and the Greek city-states in which he had grown up. Some people criticise Paul for not questioning the institution of slavery; but if you read the Letter to Philemon, which we are considering in this chapter, and take it seriously, then slavery cannot survive. Now you may object at this point that it was not until the nineteenth century that Christians in general reached the view that they had to oppose slavery. That is true, and may serve to remind us how slow we are to question institutions in which our economic or other comfort is involved. For Paul, because of his passionate involvement with Christ, individuals mattered; it was of no concern to him whether they were slaves or members of the upper classes. If institutions dehumanised people, then it was self-evident to him that they were evil, although we must admit that the idea of 'institutions' and their tendency to undermine the deepest values of humanity, was not the kind of discourse to which Paul and his generation were given.

The Letter to Philemon

What we shall do for the first half of this chapter is to read the shortest and therefore the last of the letters in the Pauline canon – the Letter to Philemon. It is short enough to read the entire text; and because in most Christian lectionaries Philemon only appears once a year, on a Saturday, when no one ever goes to church, it is also a letter that is unfamiliar to many Christians.

The letter is artfully constructed, and carefully composed. Philemon, the addressee, is being asked for a favour by Paul, and it is only fair to warn you that some critics think that Paul is being disgracefully manipulative here. You must make up your mind about this as you read, but I shall suggest another way of reading it. We shall simply go through the entire letter, commenting on the way:

> (1-3) Paul, a prisoner of Jesus Christ, and Timothy, our fellow Christian, to Philemon, our beloved fellow-worker, and to Apphia our fellow Christian and to Archippus our fellow soldier, and to the church in your house, grace to you and peace, from God our Father and from the Lord Jesus Christ.

As always, Paul starts by identifying himself; and, as so often, he presents a co-author, Timothy, whom we know well from other letters and from Acts. However, we shall not guess from the remainder of the letter that Timothy had anything whatever to do with this composition. The word that I have translated as 'fellow Christian', incidentally, is 'brother' in the case of Timothy, and 'sister' in the case of Apphia, who may perhaps be Mrs Philemon.

So although the letter is addressed to Philemon, and it is of him that the favour is being requested, it is not precisely a private letter; in addition to Apphia and Archippus, the intended audience includes 'the church in your house'. We may perhaps imagine this being read out at the Sunday gathering and imagine Philemon's reactions as it goes on.

The greeting is one that we have seen in very many of Paul's letters, and it needs to be given its full weight. None of Paul's solutions to the pastoral problems that he dealt with is comprehensible unless it is placed into the context of his basic insights about the story of God, whom he had learned to call 'Father', and the place of his beloved Jesus in that story:

> (4-7) I give thanks to my God all the time
> as I make mention of you in my prayers,
> when I hear of the love and faith that you
> have for the Lord Jesus, and for all the
> saints, [my prayer is] that the solidarity of
> your faith may become active in the

> recognition of every good thing that is
> among us [leading us] to Christ. For I had
> much joy and comfort because of your
> love, because the bowels of the saints have
> been given rest by you, my brother.

As I say, Paul has a big favour to ask of Philemon, but he has not yet revealed what this favour might be. Paul here follows his normal template, and that of letters in general in the ancient world, by having a 'thanksgiving' quite early on, asserting his gratitude to God for what Philemon has done. Or rather, not done, precisely: Paul describes it as 'faith and love for the Lord Jesus', two members of the triad that we have seen elsewhere in Paul. These two are directed, as always in Paul, towards his beloved Lord Jesus; but if you love Jesus, it follows for Paul that you must also love his 'saints', who are, to repeat, not the dead, but the living who have proclaimed that Jesus is their 'Lord'.

Now, perhaps, Philemon may start to guess what is being asked of him; for Paul's prayer has a particular intention. The ideas of 'faith' and 'love' are repeated in the second half of the sentence; and faith is qualified by the very Pauline notion of 'solidarity'; the Greek word here is *koinonia*, which can mean things like union, partnership, fellowship, association, participation, even communion – but I quite like the idea of 'solidarity' as a translation. It is the quality of opening out, in particular to one's fellow Christians, and (as Paul indicates here) recognising goodness in them, as part of the journey 'to Christ'. And Paul uses a phrase here to commend the way Philemon has in the past extended *koinonia* to his fellow Christians, which I have translated, somewhat crudely, as 'giving rest to the bowels of the saints'; we shall encounter this idea again in the course of the letter. The sentence reaches a climax with the vocative 'my brother'; and it is not impossible that Philemon may by now be shifting uncomfortably in his seat, as it dawns on him that a difficult request is going to be made of him:

> (8-16) Therefore, even though I have the confidence to command you [to do] what is fitting, I should rather beg you, because of [your] love, being, as I am, Paul, an old man – and now a prisoner of Christ Jesus – I am begging you with regard to my child, whom I have fathered in prison: Onesimus, who was once **useless** to you, but is now **useful** (both to you and to me), whom I sent to you, him, that is to say, my bowels, whom I wished to keep by me, in order that on your behalf he might be of service to me in my gospel-imprisonment; but, without your consent, I didn't want to do anything, not wishing your good deed to be under compulsion, but rather voluntary. Perhaps this was the reason why he was separated from you for a while, that you might have him back for eternity, no longer as a slave,

> but as something more than a slave, a
> beloved fellow Christian, beloved especially
> for me – but how much more beloved for
> you, both in the flesh and in the Lord!

Now we (and Philemon, perhaps) can start to see something of what Paul is up to here. He is unafraid to exert, or at least refer to, his undoubted authority as a Christian leader; and whatever the request is, it is 'fitting' and something that Paul could reasonably 'command'. But he wants it to be done out of the 'love' on which Paul has already congratulated Philemon. Then Paul angles for Philemon's sympathy, drawing his audience's attention to the fact that he is not only an old man, but also in prison (and we notice how he cannot avoid mentioning his beloved Christ Jesus); cleverly he uses a word that avoids any hint of giving orders, 'I am begging', to give Philemon at least the illusion that he has something of a choice in the matter.

What is the request on which we are eavesdropping? It concerns 'my child', a phrase at which Philemon and the church in his house might raise a questioning eyebrow, 'whom I have fathered in prison' (literally, 'in chains'). Only then, and at the last possible moment, is this 'child' named as Onesimus, a name that means something like 'useful' or 'profitable'. Now Philemon knows what is going on; if, that is to say, he did not already know it – for it is possible that it was Onesimus who had actually carried this letter from Paul to Philemon. The most likely reading of this text is that

Onesimus is a runaway slave, belonging to Philemon, who had come to visit Paul in his prison, and that Paul had there received him as a Christian (although it is only fair to admit to you that some other scholars read the text in a somewhat less dramatic way). You should also know that the penalties for runaway slaves were severe in this world, and involved branding, flogging, cutting off the miscreant's ears, and capital punishment. So Paul (and Onesimus for that matter) is taking a very great risk.

Now Paul makes a double pun on Onesimus' name, when he speaks of **useless** and **useful**. It is a double pun because although it comes from a different root, it is clearly a play on the name; and it also plays on the name of Paul's (and Philemon's) beloved Christ: for the words here are *achrestos* and *euchrestos*, which would have sounded, as it was read out in the church, like 'un-Christ' and 'well-Christ', or 'unchristian' and 'properly Christian'. Philemon cannot have been in any doubt of the point that Paul was making to him.

If he was in any such doubt, the reference to 'bowels' will have made it clear. He has already been congratulated on 'giving rest to the bowels of the saints'; now he has precisely such a 'bowel' (my apologies for the unremitting use of this term, but it serves to make the point) in the shape of his runaway slave.

Once again, Paul angles for sympathy; he might have kept Onesimus with him, to look after him (on Philemon's behalf!) in prison, but wanted his owner to *choose* to do good, not be compelled into it. At this point, very delicately, Paul touches on the fact that Onesimus has run away; indeed, he does it so delicately that we cannot be certain that running away is what has happened here. Paul speaks of it as 'being separated'; and what he does here is to place the whole episode into its proper setting as part of the story of what God is doing. The word for 'separated' is a divine passive, which in this dialect of Greek carries the implication that it was actually God at work doing the separation, in order for Philemon to have him back, but with the Onesimus story told differently now, 'no longer a slave, but something more than a slave, a beloved fellow Christian'. And if Philemon finds himself just itching to reach for the branding-iron, the whip, or a sword to chop off this wretched slave's head or ears, then he will be given pause by the next line: 'beloved especially for me – but how much more beloved for you, both in the flesh and in the Lord'. Philemon has been commended for his love, and clearly has a very good relationship with Paul; and now he has to see this wretched possession of his (for that is what slavery means) as a beloved brother! We may imagine the eyes of those in his house-church turned upon Philemon, to see how the letter is going down with him:

> (17-20) If you consider me your partner, accept him as though it were me. If he has done you any injustice, or if he owes you anything, put it down to my account.
> **I Paul am writing this in my own hand:**

> **I'll pay it back**. I make no mention of the fact that you owe yourself to me. Yes, my brother, let me have some **profit** from you in the Lord. Give rest to my bowels in Christ.

This is a masterpiece of language. The word I have translated as 'partner' is connected with our old friend *koinonia*, an appeal to the solidarity or communion that exists between Paul and Philemon. And if Philemon is to accept Onesimus as though it were Paul, then he must leave the branding-iron, the whip, and the sword exactly where they are. Then he continues the pun on the name of Onesimus ('profitable'), by imagining the account book open before them, and offers to pay back Philemon for any losses that he has incurred. Then, as he often does in other letters (see 1 Corinthians 16:21; Galatians 6:11; Colossians 4:18; 2 Thessalonians 3:17), Paul seizes the pen from his hapless secretary and writes his own message, underlining what he is saying. And he cannot resist a final twist, referring to what Philemon owes him, presumably the fact of his conversion to Christ.

Then come two more word-plays. The word that I have translated as **profit** is connected in Greek with the name Onesimus; and then, for the last time in the letter, Paul uses the idea of 'giving rest to bowels', and it is quite clear now what he is expecting Philemon to do (or to refrain from doing: branding, flogging, killing). And the last phrase of all? Inevitably (for this is Paul) 'in Christ':

> (21-22) I write to you, confident in your obedience, knowing that you will do even more than what I am saying. And at the same time make a guest room ready for me, for I am hoping, through your prayers, to be given to you as a gift.

Poor Philemon! It is inconceivable (isn't it?) that he could have refused Paul's carefully crafted request. Here is the passing reference to 'obedience', to a command that (as he has already indicated) he might have made, but carefully didn't, and indicating that he expects his brother in the Lord to do even more than what is being asked for. Then, just in case the desire to give Onesimus what he deserves is getting the upper hand, Paul indicates that soon Philemon may have to deal with the author in person, with the suggestion about making a 'guest room ready', and the ready assumption that Philemon is praying for Paul's release from prison, and would welcome such an outcome:

> (23-25) Epaphras my fellow prisoner greets you in Christ Jesus, Mark, Aristarchus, Demas, and Luke, my co-workers [greet you]. The grace of the Lord Jesus Christ be with the spirit of you [all].

So the letter ends, with another reminder that this is not a private communication: five fellow Christians are in on it at Paul's end, and the last line uses the plural form of you (which I have tried to indicate by the use of '[all]'), although the rest of the letter has been addressed to Philemon in person, to recall us to the fact that it is being read out to the entire church in Philemon's house. The ending is characteristic of Paul; but you may like to imagine Philemon asking what the 'grace' (free gift, unconditional love) of the Lord Jesus Christ might imply in his response to this letter. (Put that branding iron down, now!)

What was Philemon's response to this request? What would yours have been? Two facts may be of interest. In the first place, the letter has been preserved. If Philemon had opted to ignore Paul's request, it might simply have ended up in the waste-paper basket. Secondly, Ignatius of Antioch, at the end of the first century and beginning of the second, knows of an Onesimus who was bishop of Ephesus. Could that be the runaway slave, unflogged and unbranded, who had nervously carried the letter from Paul in prison to his angry master? Well it could, though there is not a shred of evidence for it. And it may even be, as some scholars have suggested, that Onesimus was the person responsible for collecting Paul's letters, and perhaps even circulating Ephesians as a kind of introduction to Paul's thought. The fact is that we don't know; and we must be grateful that this remarkable letter was preserved at all for us to read in our time and place.

But what about slavery?

Now at this point, you may be rising up in your wrath, and muttering that it is all very well for Paul to be lavishing his favours on this one slave, who has become a Christian and been nice to Paul in his cell; but should not Paul have been demonstrating outside the Roman emperor's palace for an end to slavery? Well, it is hard to mount a demonstration if you are a prisoner; but the charge is worth considering, for all that.

The question must be raised, of course, for slavery is a terrible thing for humans to do to each other, and you might expect Christians, including St Paul, to have something to say about it. There are two obvious points to make in Paul's defence. The first is simply that he may never have thought of it; slavery was part of the world that he inhabited, and it may not have crossed his mind that there was anything to be done about it. A generation ago, for example, those who showed the level of eco-sensitivity that we nowadays take for granted, would have been dismissed as tree-hugging eccentrics. None of us knows what our grandchildren will find to reproach us with, aspects of the way we live today that we simply take for granted, but which they will regard as outrageous.

The second is that (although we have not made much of it in this book) Paul often sounds as though he thinks that the world might end at any minute; and if that is the case, then doing something about structures of injustice might seem like 'rearranging the deckchairs on the Titanic', as the saying goes.

Some Pauline texts

We can go a bit further than this, however. Paul does

talk about slavery elsewhere, and we can examine some of these texts, to see what attitude he might adopt to the institution of slavery today.

The first one is in 1 Corinthians 7:20–24:

> Let each [of you] remain in the calling in which you were called. Were you called as a slave? Don't worry about it, but even if you can become free, it is better to use it. For the one who is called in the Lord as a slave is a freedman of the Lord. Likewise, the free person who is called is a slave of Christ. You were bought at a price; don't become slaves of human beings. Brothers and sisters, let each of you remain in the calling in which you were called, in God's presence.

The general context is that 'the times are shortened' (7:29), and so the Corinthians are not to seek to change their status. So the unmarried should remain unmarried, except in certain circumstances (7:9), and the married should remain married, except in certain circumstances (15). Likewise the circumcised and the uncircumcised (18–19); and so, apparently, with slaves, although it has to be said that the line 'it is better to use it' might be understood either as meaning 'use the chance of becoming free' or 'use the chance that your status as slave gives you'. Either way, Paul's argument serves to relativise the institution of slavery, for 'in the Lord' for Paul is short-hand for being a Christian. So if you are a slave, you are in fact a freedman (a slave who has been given, or has purchased, their liberty); and if you are a Christian who has obtained or never lost freedom, then you are 'a slave of Christ', a title that Paul proudly arrogates to himself in Romans 1:1. Then, once again, Paul reaches for the metaphor of 'redemption', an idea that has gone dead on us, but means the extraordinarily generous act of buying a slave and then giving them their freedom as a gift. This is what Paul refers to when he says 'you were bought at a price'. And the whole thing is 'in God's presence', so that your social status really does not matter. If we take this line of argument seriously, then the institution of slavery really cannot survive: because those who are slaves are, for Paul, human beings with their own dignity and rights, and therefore may not be bought and sold.

The same is true of the next three texts, Colossians 3:22–4:1; Ephesians 6:5–9; and 1 Timothy 6:1–2. They all come from what are known as 'household codes', giving advice about how to organise family living in the body of Christ. We shall take the Colossians passage first:

> Slaves, obey in every respect those who are
> your 'lords' according to the flesh, not by
> way of 'eye-slavery', like people who are
> trying to please human beings, but in
> sincerity of heart, fearing the 'Lord'.
> Whatever you do, do it from the heart, as

> for the 'Lord', and not for human beings,
> knowing that it is from the 'Lord' that you
> will receive the recompense of your
> inheritance. Be slaves of the 'Lord' Christ.
> For the one who commits injustice will
> receive the reward for the injustice they
> have committed, and there is no awareness
> of status; 'lords' give your slaves what is
> just and equitable, knowing that you also
> have a 'Lord' in heaven.

This is actually a very clever piece of writing. At one level, it allows the institution of slavery to continue in the new dispensation, and so offers no ammunition to those who regard Christianity as a fundamentally anarchist organisation, which marks 'the end of civilisation as we know it'. Actually, of course, that is precisely what it does mark; but Paul allows his Christians to work this out for themselves. For at a deeper level, you should notice how the author uses the word 'lord' and 'Lord'. For Paul there is only one 'Lord', namely Jesus Christ; and so when he speaks of slave-owners as 'lords', their status is inevitably relativised. So slaves are told to obey their 'lords', but to give their fear, or reverence, to the 'Lord', the only one who matters. Paul recognises the possibility of injustice on the part of slave masters, but reassures his people that the injustice will be redressed. Then comes the devastating remark that 'there is no awareness of status'. If everyone is equal before the Lord, then all human constructs are relativised. If that is so, then the institution of slavery does not really matter. If we find that an odd doctrine, then we must try to put ourselves in that other and very different world that was Colossae in the first century AD. And see how at the end of the passage the author turns to the slave masters, and, very delicately, reminds them that they have their own 'Lord', before whom they will have to give an account of themselves. No one who read this text carefully could possibly justify the institution of slavery.

Ephesians 6:5–9 is another step in this direction:

> Slaves, obey those who are your 'lords' according to the flesh, with fear and trembling in sincerity of heart, not by way of 'eye-slavery', like people who are trying to please human beings, but as slaves of Christ, doing the will of God with all your heart, living out your slavery with enthusiasm, for the 'Lord', and not for human beings, knowing that each of you, if you do good, will obtain the same from the 'Lord', whether you are a slave or a free person. And you 'lords', do the same for them, give up threats, knowing that their 'Lord' and your 'lord' is in heaven. And he has no awareness of status.

These two passages are clearly connected, whether because they come from the same author, or because one is dependent on the other, or because they have both been influenced by some third treatise on the Christian treatment of slaves. There is no need to pursue that question; but it is worth noting how Ephesians strengthens the case against the slave owners. 'Slaves' are slaves of Christ, (for the 'Lord'); and the warning to slave owners is a good deal sharper, reminding them as it does that slaves and the free are equal before their real 'Lord'. And the line about awareness of status in this treatment of the matter is presented as the climax. Once again, if you read this text carefully, you cannot possibly justify slavery in terms of Christianity.

The same can be argued, though with perhaps greater difficulty, of our remaining text, 1 Timothy 6:1–2:

> As many of you as are slaves under the
> yoke, think of your own masters as worthy
> of all honour, **in order that God's name
> and teaching may not be defamed**.
> Those who have masters who are believers
> are not to despise them, because they are
> your fellow Christians; rather, live out your
> slavery, because they are believers and
> beloved, who devote themselves to doing
> good [it is only fair to warn you that this
> could be translated: because those who benefit
> by the service are believers and beloved].

At first sight, this passage may seem to have accommodated itself a little too readily to the *status quo*; here it is only slaves who are addressed. Their masters are not instructed to behave in a Christian manner, but the slaves are instructed to pay them honour, and not to despise them. Where, you cry, is the Christian equality in all this? Not so fast, however.

Notice, first, that slaves are addressed; and that in itself is a matter for astonishment. They are treated as human beings, who can make decisions about their own conduct. Secondly, see what the basic reason for the exhortation is: **in order that God's name and teaching may not be defamed.** It is all about the proclamation of the gospel. Paul, or whoever wrote this letter, has no desire for the good news about Jesus to be hampered by irrelevant considerations (another age, of course, might not have regarded a critique of slavery as entirely foreign to the gospel – but ours is indeed another age, and has its own set of problems).

And it is an odd temptation against which the slaves are warned, that they might 'despise' their masters. You do not get the sense here that slaves are an inferior class, beneath consideration; and, of course, there is a covert, but unmistakable warning to slave owners, in the statement that they 'devote themselves to doing good', and that they are 'believers and beloved'. If slave owners are to live up to these words, then they are going to have to change.

Conclusion: in Paul's gospel, people matter

In the end, there is no getting away from it, people matter for Paul. Once you have seen the truth about

Jesus, then all those for whom Jesus died are persons with their own dignity and human rights, and equally deserving of respect. We may conclude this chapter with a few texts that make this point unmistakably.

Sometimes respect for persons can have rather shocking consequences. Consider (as we have suggested before) the reaction of Jewish hearers who have been nodding in approval at Paul's denunciation of the Gentiles in chapter 1 of Romans, and who then find themselves addressed in these uncompromising terms:

> So you have no excuse, my friend, whoever
> you are who judges. For on that precise point
> on which you judge your neighbour, you
> condemn your own self – for you who do
> the judging do the very same things yourself.
>
> *Romans 2:1*

There is a similar shock implied when Paul realises (and communicates his realisation to the new Christians) that Gentiles also belong in God's story (Romans 1:16; 2:9–10); the idea contained in 'Jew first and then Gentile' is deeply subversive. Or consider this passage, where Paul speaks of the effect of baptism; that it puts an end to all humanly contrived artificial distinctions:

> You see, as many of you as are baptised
> into Christ, have put on Christ. There is

> [in Christ] no such thing as Jew or Gentile,
> no such thing as slave or free, no such thing
> as male and female.   *Galatians 3:27–28*

This is an astonishingly radical understanding of God's new story. The point is that all human beings are equal under God, a doctrine that for a time was neglected in South Africa; but all human beings tend to behave this way when we want to defend our own interests. This is what makes surprising the passage in Romans 13:1–7 that we have already looked at, where Paul insists on the importance of obeying secular authority. And even there we should notice that Paul frames it with his insistence on the importance of all human beings (13:8):

> Don't owe anyone anything, except to love
> one another; for the one who loves the Other
> has fulfilled the Law.

So Paul is very insistent with the Romans that they must cope with the tensions within their church by not condemning one another (14:13–15), with regard to questions about what is and is not profane eating:

> So – put an end to mutual condemnation.
> Instead, make this the subject of your
> judgement, not to put an obstacle or a
> stumbling block in the way of your fellow
> Christian. I know, and I am persuaded in

> the Lord Jesus, that nothing is profane of
> itself; but if someone thinks that something
> is profane, then it is profane for them.
> But if your fellow Christian is caused pain
> because of [your] diet, you are no longer
> acting in accordance with the principle
> of love. Don't let your diet cause the
> destruction of the person for whom
> Christ died.

Paul is diplomatically trying to deal here with the problems of a church that he has yet to visit, and has not founded; but they may well have found his solution rather shocking. Human respect is based on the things that *really* matter, not what you eat or where you purify the vessels after communion. Nor is it a matter of gaining other people's good opinion, but of consideration for fellow Christians, as he indicates when trying to sort out the difficult question of whether the Corinthians were permitted to eat food offered to idols:

> For if someone sees you who have
> 'knowledge' banqueting in an idol-house,
> won't their weak conscience be 'built up'
> and make them eat food offered to idols?
> Your weak fellow Christian, for whom
> Christ died, is being destroyed by your
> 'knowledge'. So, when you sin against
> fellow Christians and batter their weak

> consciences, you are in fact sinning against Christ. So – if what I eat causes my fellow Christian to trip up, I shall never eat meat, ever again, so as not to make my fellow Christian stumble.
>
> *1 Corinthians 8:10–13*

The point here is that people matter more than principles, and that one's brother or sister in Christ demands our enormous respect. Once you can talk about being 'in Christ', then people take on an altogether new and momentous significance (Romans 14:15).

Do you think that Paul's stance on slavery makes sense? Why have Christians been so slow to abolish slavery? Can you be a Christian and a slave owner?

Eleven

Paul and women

It is sometimes argued that Paul is what used to be called a 'male chauvinist pig'; this chapter will seek to take issue with that stance, but will also try to be respectful towards those who feel that the Church is hostile to women, and that it is all Paul's fault.

Not that man . . .

There is a story of a nineteenth-century American woman who had been born a slave. She could not read, but her children used to read the Bible to her, since she was a Christian and loved the Bible. The only exception was when they suggested that she might like to hear something from St Paul. Her response was invariable: 'not that man'. The reason was simply that when she had been a slave, a pastor used to be brought out by the slave owner to read to the assembly those parts of St Paul that served to keep slaves and women in their places. More recently, I myself was summoned to a house where the wife was Catholic and the husband was a member of a very small Protestant denomination. He insisted that I should tell his wife that she should join his church, because 'that is what the Bible says'. When pressed on the meaning of this at first sight rather obscure utterance, he had recourse to what he took to be St Paul's views on the importance of wives obeying their husbands.

It is therefore an important question, what St Paul thought about women, since he has at times been recruited into their ranks by those who wished to keep women in their (lowly) place. It is proper to say, however, that it may not have been precisely Paul's 'question'. There are in any case three factors that we need to bear in mind when we consider this issue. The first is that Paul writes in a hurry, and with his mind on his own issues, not those of our day. The second is that things were (in his view) very likely ending quite soon, in which case there is no place for examining the status of women. The third is that the less it seemed that things were indeed ending, the more imperative it would have become to accommodate the norms of Greek and Roman society. And that was not a world in which women were especially liberated.

Some alarming texts

It is only fair to start with some of the more embarrassing texts (embarrassing, that is, for those who wish, as I do, to defend Paul against the charge of being against women). From that point of view, it may be best to begin with 1 Corinthians 14:33–36, which various male authorities have gleefully flung at women who appeared to be getting above themselves in matters ecclesial:

> As in all the churches of the saints,
> let the women be silent in the churches;

> for it is not permitted for them to speak.
> Instead, let them be subordinated, just as
> the Law says. If they want to learn
> something, let them ask their own
> husbands at home; for it is a disgrace for a
> woman to speak in the assembly. Or was it
> from you people that God's word emerged?
> Or did it come only to you?

This comes in a context (chapters 12–14) where Paul is trying to bring some order into what appears to have been a somewhat tempestuous liturgy in Corinth. It has, we must admit, frequently been used to indicate that women may not preach in church (or assembly). The difficulty is that we do not, and Paul's Corinthians presumably did, know what the problem was. If the general context is one of liturgical disorder, then it is possible that the women had been calling out in the assembly questions like 'What did he say?', 'What is he on about?', and you can understand that this might have had somewhat chaotic effects. On the other hand, Paul's grammar at the end makes it clear that the two rhetorical questions with which he concludes are not addressed to the women, but to the whole Corinthian church, since the 'you people' is masculine. What we are not permitted to do is to deduce from Paul's treatment of a (perhaps rather urgently untidy) Corinthian situation to how he might have legislated for us in this century and in this country (wherever and whenever you are reading these words). Paul, it cannot be too often emphasised, would be very surprised to think of us reading his words today, and in this place. He is solving the problems in Corinth, two decades after the death of Jesus; he would probably prefer us to solve our own problems for ourselves.

The reference to the Law is presumably to Genesis 3:16, where after the scene in the garden Eve is told 'your desire shall be for your husband, and he shall lord it over you'; but here we may assume that Paul is reaching for a scriptural argument to make the point that he needs to make. We may not assume without further ado that Paul has for all time and in all places ruled out the possibility of any woman opening her mouth in church.

Then there are the household codes, of which the following passages (Colossians 3:18; Ephesians 5:21–25; 1 Timothy 2:11–15) may be taken as representative:

Colossians   Wives, be **subordinated** to your husbands, as is fitting in the Lord. Husbands, love your wives, and don't get bitter against them.

Ephesians   ... being **subordinated** to each other in reverence for Christ, wives [**subordinated**] to your own husbands, for the husband is head of the wife, just as Christ is head of the church, but he is Saviour of the body. No – just as the Church is **subordinated** to Christ, so let

> the women be [**subordinated**] to their husbands in every respect. Husbands, love your wives, just as Christ loved the Church, and gave himself up for her ...

1 Timothy
> Let a wife/woman learn in peace, in all **subordination**. I do not permit a woman to teach, nor to have authority over a man, but to be at peace. For Adam was fashioned first, and then Eve. And it was not Adam who was deceived; it was the woman who was deceived and so committed the transgression. But she will be saved through child-bearing, if they remain in faith and love and holiness, along with decency.

Well you were warned that there are some alarming texts. What can we say about all this? Firstly, it would be possible to argue that many scholars regard all three of these as coming from a later hand than Paul's, not just because they want to defend Paul, but on other grounds as well; that, however, may strike you as a rather craven way of evading the plain facts of the case. If Paul did not write these words, then at least somebody, living not very long after him, thought that this is what he would be saying 'if he were alive today'.

Secondly, you may have noticed the keywords 'subordinate/subordination' appearing in each of the above passages. There may be a clue here (even if the argument might seem less weighty to our ears, it was perhaps self-evident to a contemporary of Paul's) that creation comes graded: God, Christ, men, women, the rest. If that is so, then his use of terms of that kind would be an attempt to preserve what God has done in creation.

Thirdly, all but the last of these three passages suffers from internal subversion. No sooner have the husbands listening to the Colossians passage elbowed their wives, asking, 'Did you hear what the man said?' than the wives turn on them and quote what husbands are supposed to do. In the text from Ephesians, the message is even stronger: husbands are to give themselves up for their wives, precisely as Christ gave himself up for the Church. This is the ultimate in self-sacrifice, and makes impossible any notion that husbands are more important than their wives, although I suppose that you might argue that the text implies that, as Christ is superior to the Church, so the husband is superior to the wife, which we should find a bit embarrassing. In the third citation, one has to admit, there is less room for manoeuvre. Now we do not (for sure) know who wrote this passage, and therefore we have no idea about the situation into which he was talking, so we shall be unwise to adopt any particular attitudes; therefore, beyond noting that the author is employing arguments from Scripture that we may find less than convincing, it is perhaps best to say nothing at this point.

What is going on here?
1 Corinthians 11:2–16 and a possible clue

What we have to do above all is listen to what Paul is saying. A very helpful passage is the famous (one might wish to say 'notorious') section in 1 Corinthians 11. At first blush, this can seem utterly repressive of women; but a more reflective reading indicates that there is more to it than first meets the eye. The arguments that Paul employs need some attention, and I have tried to separate them out with Roman numerals:

> I commend you on the grounds that in every respect you remember me, and that you preserve the traditions, just as I handed them down to you.
>
> 1. But I want you people to be well aware that Christ is the head of every male, and that the male is the head of the female, and that God is the head of Christ.
>
> 2. Every man who prays or prophesies with something on his head, shames his head. Every woman who prays or prophesies with her head uncovered, shames her head. For it is just the same as though her head were shaved. You see, if a woman is not covered, let her have her hair cut off. But if it is a

dishonour for a woman to have her head shaved or her hair cut off, let her be covered. You see, a man ought not to have his head covered, since he is the image and glory of God. But the woman is the glory of the man.

3. For it is not the man who came out of the woman, but the woman out of the man. And it was not the man who was created on the woman's account, but the woman on the man's account.

4. This is the reason why the woman ought to have **authority** over her head – because of the angels.

4a. However, there is no woman apart from the man, and no man apart from the woman in the Lord, because just as the woman is from the man, so the man is through the woman. But everything comes from God.

5. Reach a verdict among yourselves: is it appropriate for a woman to pray to God when she is not covered? Does not Nature herself teach you that if a man has long hair, that is a dishonour for him? And if a woman has long hair, that is glory for her? Because long hair is given her as a covering.

6. But if anyone is disposed to pick a
   fight, we have no custom of this sort,
   nor do the churches of God.

It is hard to be sure whether we have accurately distinguished the several arguments that Paul uses; but what is clear is that he thinks it really important to get the matter properly sorted out in Corinth, and to that end he produces several different arguments.

What, for Paul, would count as 'getting the matter properly sorted out'? It is clearly something to do with how the women are dressing, and, more precisely, something to do with what happens on their heads. The word that I have printed as **authority** means just that, but for understandable reasons Jerome translated it into Latin as 'veil', and so, in my lifetime, Catholic women had to go veiled into church. As children, whenever we entered a church, if my mother or sister did not have a mantilla with them, we had to lend them our grubby handkerchiefs, all because of this passage. Once again, we have to say that Paul would have been entirely surprised at this turn of events; he was trying to solve a problem in Corinth in the 50s AD, not the United Kingdom (of which he had never heard) in the 1950s.

We have therefore to walk carefully here, and try to listen to what he is saying. Let us walk through the several arguments (and I have to admit that not all scholars agree on how many there are).

1. This argument is a standard one for Paul, and would probably not have raised many eyebrows in his world, though it does not carry much weight in our culture. It assumes a descending ladder that goes: God-Christ-man-woman. And the way Paul here presents it suggests that it would have found ready acceptance in Corinth.

2. This argument presumably contains the state of affairs that Paul was trying to bring about: if women pray or prophesy, they must do it with heads covered, whereas men are to pray or prophesy with heads uncovered. Incidentally, as we move on, we may notice that Paul assumes as a matter of course that men and women have the same liturgical function: *both* are expected to 'pray or prophesy'. But the argument here deployed in support of this position is one that defeats us today and in our cultural location: a woman praying with head uncovered is like a woman with her hair cut off. Paul takes it for granted that this is an undesirable state of affairs.

3. This is an argument from Scripture, specifically from Genesis 2:18–23, the second account of creation, where the woman is created precisely so that the man should not be alone, and from a rib taken from the man's side.

4. The next argument concerns 'angels'. Once more, we must assume that those who heard this letter read out in Corinth will have understood a great

deal more than we do. Various suggestions have been made about the angels: they might have been those referred to in Genesis 6:2–4, when the 'sons of God' (often understood as angels) fell in love with the 'daughters of humans', with catastrophic results. Other scholars refer to a text in the Dead Sea Scrolls (the 'War Scroll'), which urges purity on the sectaries in the camp before the final battle, because the angels are fighting on their side.

4a. At this point, Paul remembers his basic doctrine of the equality of men and women, and insists on the balance between the sexes, using two telling phrases, of great importance to him; 'in the Lord', and 'from God'. All Paul's arguing in the end goes back to those two stable points of his creed, to Jesus and to the Father.

5. The next argument is from Natural Law, and is presumably intended to be decisive. The Corinthian Christians are invited simply to look at the facts of the case and see it for themselves: women should have their heads covered, men should not have long hair, but women should. The word translated as 'covering', as a function of woman's hair, could also be understood as a 'chastity belt'. At this point, we simply have to admit that we do not know quite enough about Paul's Corinth to be sure what is going on here.

6. The final argument may hint at a lack of certainty on Paul's part. It is an argument from authority,

and from the practice of the Christian churches round the Mediterranean, and has a touch of despair about it.

What is going on here? As I say, it is hard to be sure, but a few basic considerations may be helpful. In the first place, scholars point out that Paul is emotionally involved here. In his judgement, something is going on that simply ought not to be; and there are those who guess that some of the women in Corinth were going in for what nowadays is called 'cross-dressing', women dressing as men, perhaps combining that with a homosexual lifestyle. That may be so; in the nature of the case, we cannot be sure, but we should notice that Paul's blood pressure is rising at this point.

Another point that may be worth mentioning is that there was a fear in the Greek culture of women getting too ecstatic in their religious practice. Euripides' great play, *The Bacchae*, presents us with the women of Thebes, worshippers of Dionysius. The story of these redoubtable ladies ended with their leader Agave killing her son Pentheus, the somewhat humourless King of Thebes, under the supposition that he was a mountain lion. It may well be that when Paul speaks of women having **authority** over their heads, he is trying to discourage precisely that sort of expression of emotionalism in religion that Pentheus so strongly resisted, and which in the end was the death of him.

However, we have to admit that we are only guessing here; at all events, it is, or should be, clear that we shall not be on safe ground if we build any inner-church legislation on this passage. Paul may be in something of a muddle here, and we don't really know what the issue was in Corinth.

Paul's radical stance

There is one very important passage where Paul indicates what he thinks Christ has done for us; and this has implications for the all-important question of Paul's attitude to women. In Galatians, he is arguing that by giving in to the blandishments of the spin-doctors from Jerusalem that they should observe kosher regulations, circumcision, and Jewish festivals, the Christians of those parts are going back on the freedom that Christ came to give them. In 3:27–28 he argues:

> ... for as many of you as were baptised
> into Christ have put on Christ; there is [in
> Christ] no such thing as Jew or Gentile, no
> such thing as slave or free, no such thing as
> male and female.

The point here is that all the artificial divisions between human beings simply do not obtain in Christ; all of us are adopted sons and daughters of God, and therefore our conventional views of status, whether based on ethnic-religious (Jew or Gentile), class (slave or free), or gender considerations (male and female), are simply passé. Christ represents the equality of all humanity, and therefore all are equal before God. Incidentally, you may have noticed that whereas Paul speaks here of 'Jew *or* Gentile . . . slave *or* free', when we get to the third of the contrasting pairs, it is 'male *and* female', which makes it a clear reference to Genesis 1:27 'male and female he created them'. So his position is very radical indeed.

Nor is there any evidence that Paul ever went back on that. It is true that he never quite repeats that triad again, possibly, as some scholars have suggested, because of trouble with the women in Corinth. So at 1 Corinthians 12:13, in the exhortation to unity, we feel the absence of 'male and female' when we hear the reader proclaim:

> . . . you see, by one Spirit, all of us were baptised into one body, whether Jews or Greeks, whether slaves or free, and we were all given to drink of the one Spirit.

And in Colossians 3:11 we have, in a context of the new life that we are to live, the following range:

> putting on the new person, the one that is being renewed, according to the likeness of the one who created him, where there is no Greek and Jew, circumcision and uncircumcision, barbarian, Scythian, slave, free – no: Christ is all in all.

The point here is that Christ has restored the God-likeness of humanity, and that means that the artificial divisions into which humanity divides itself are abolished; but men and women are not mentioned.

Likewise at Romans 10:12, we hear, in a context where Paul is asserting that Gentiles belong equally with Jews in God's story, the same lack:

> ... for there is no distinction between Jew
> and Greek, for the same one is Lord of all.

It is of course odd that Paul does not use the opportunity to reassert the equality of men and women here, but, as I say, it is possible that he had his fingers badly burned at Corinth, and in any case, his focus here is on the relationship between Jew and non-Jew in the story of God. There is no evidence at all, however, that he retreated from his basic position of the equality of all humanity.

Paul's fellow-workers

We can in fact go a bit further than this, and point to Paul's esteem for women whom he regarded as fellow-workers for the gospel. A good place to look is Romans 16, where Paul, engaged in his diplomatic mission to a church that he did not know well, but needed to get on his side, gives a long list of people whom he wishes to greet in Rome. The point here is that he wants the Romans to be aware that he is known to quite a lot of them. This is not a well-known text; compilers of lectionaries tend to think of it as too boring to be read out in church:

> I commend to you our fellow Christian Phoebe, who is deacon of the church in Cenchreae, that you may give her hospitality in the Lord appropriate to the saints, and furnish her with anything that she needs. For she is a benefactress to many people, including myself.

From these lines it actually looks possible that it was Phoebe who brought this most influential of Paul's letters to Rome. Certainly, Paul holds her in very high regard, calling her 'deacon' of the church at Cenchreae. This place was the easternmost port of Corinth, and therefore a site of some importance. It has to be admitted that I am pushing it a bit by calling her a 'deacon' in the translation; at this stage it could mean no more than someone who gives service, but even that is an honourable function in the Christian church, as a glance at Mark 10:45 will show. There is no mistaking Paul's esteem for this lady, and his gratitude to her. As always there is that phrase 'in the Lord', which is the solution to all problems for Paul.

In the next verse (16:3), we find a married couple, Prisca and Aquila. Despite the apparently similar grammatical form, Aquila is masculine (it means 'Eagle'), and Prisca feminine; but we notice that it is Prisca (elsewhere sometimes named as Priscilla, which is an affectionate diminutive) who is named first, and presumably wears the trousers in that household. According to Acts 18, these two were very good to Paul in Corinth, and shared his profession of tent-making. When Paul wrote 1 Corinthians (see 16:19) they were with him in Ephesus; so they get around, and have now returned to Rome, from which city they had been expelled, presumably by Claudius' decree in AD 49 (see Acts 18:2).

Immediately after them (and some very strong praise of them in verses 4–5), we hear in Romans 16:6 about 'Maria, who has laboured a great deal in your regard'. This could be a Latin name, the feminine of Marius, or it could be the nearest a writer of Greek could get to Miriam, the name of the mother of Jesus. We notice that this lady is described in the following terms, which are highly laudatory for Paul:

> who has laboured a great deal in your regard.

Then comes what is almost certainly a husband-and-wife team, like Prisca and Aquila:

> Greet Andronicus and Junia, my kinsfolk
> and fellow prisoners, who are conspicuous
> among the apostles, who were in Christ
> before me.
>
> *Romans 16:7*

Many translations take Junia as a man's name, Junias, which is not attested in the epigraphical evidence that we have. The reason they do this is perhaps a reluctance to accept that a woman (and Junia is a well-attested woman's name) could possibly have been a 'conspicuous ... apostle', but that is what Paul appears to say here.

The next women to be mentioned are quite interesting:

> Greet Tryphaena and Tryphosa, who have laboured in the Lord. Greet the beloved Persis [clearly a woman's name], who has laboured much in the Lord. Greet Rufus the elect one in the Lord, and his mother and mine.
> *Romans 16:12–13*

Notice that the first three here are described as having 'laboured', which is high praise in Paul's vocabulary. Tryphaena and Tryphosa are thought to be sisters; and it is a charming thought that their names might be taken to mean something like 'Dismal' and 'Droopy', so there may be some affectionate leg-pulling on Paul's part. Persis has a Greek name; but the grammar makes it clear that it is a woman. And so, of course, must be the mother of Rufus. There is an interesting train of thought here. For Rufus is mentioned in Mark's gospel as one of the two sons of Simon of Cyrene, who was forced into helping Jesus carry his cross (Mark 15:21), and the fact that Mark mentions Rufus (and his brother Alexander) suggests that he was known to Mark's community; and Mark's community is often located in Rome. So it is just possible that we are talking here of the same Rufus; in which case his mother would have been none other than Mrs Simon of Cyrene, the wife of that conscripted African.

Finally (verse 15) there is Julia, and Nereus' sister. Paul says nothing whatever about these two, but they are inescapably women, and clearly Paul holds them in esteem. There is nothing in Paul that says that women have no place in the church, and, indeed, he regards several of them as very hard workers, and clearly applauds them as such.

You may notice that Rufus' mother and Nereus' sister are not named, possibly because Paul assumes that everyone will know them, possibly because their names have for the moment slipped his mind. Many of us would feel sympathy if that is indeed the Apostle's plight.

The same is true in another passage, Philippians 4:2–3:

> I implore Evodia, and I implore Syntyche
> to have the same mindset in the Lord.

That was what he had been urging on the Philippians back in chapter 2, when he went into the hymn to Christ, having encouraged them to 'have the same mindset which was in Christ Jesus', presumably because they had not had it. And notice what he says about these two ladies:

> who have fought at my side in spreading
> the gospel.

Once again, we have here two women who are given credit for serious, and clearly energetic, work in evangelising. Paul is not one to underrate the achievements of women missionaries.

What about Mrs Paul?

The mention of Evodia and Syntyche, however, raises an interesting question. For in verse 3, Paul addresses a third member of the congregation at Philippi as 'true Syzygos', or 'true yoke-fellow'. We can probably exclude the former, since it is not attested as a name anywhere in Greek literature or inscriptions; so who is the 'yoke-fellow'? It is a metaphor from draft animals, and refers to horses or oxen who pull the plough or carts together, and is therefore a natural image for a spouse. Could Paul here be asking his wife to help ease the tension among the ladies of Philippi?

At first sight, it seems unlikely. For in 1 Corinthians 7:7 he says 'I want all human beings to be as I am', and in the next verses, 'I am saying to the unmarried and to widows, it is good for them to remain as I am. But if they are not able to be chaste, let them get married – for it is better for them to marry than to burn'. Leaving aside what we should regard as a slightly cynical theology of marriage (we shall be looking at Paul on sex in the next chapter), we have to admit that an obvious way of reading this text is to understand that Paul is talking about himself as a celibate.

It does not have to be read that way, however: it is possible that Paul means by this, especially in a place like Corinth, no more than that he wishes they could resemble him by remaining chaste, as he does when his wife is not with him. Indeed he may well be implying something of this sort at 1 Corinthians 9:4–6, when he is talking about his rights as an apostle, insisting that he has these rights, but has simply opted not to exercise them:

> Do we not have the right to eat and drink? Don't we have the right to take a Christian wife around [with us], just like the rest of the apostles, and the Lord's brothers, and Kephas? Is it just I and Barnabas who don't have the right not to work . . . ?

If there is no Mrs Paul, then his argument here does not appear to make any sense; so that could be an indicator from Paul, that he was actually married.

There is a bit more to it than this. If Luke has it right (Acts 22:3), Paul trained, as we should now say, as a rabbi, at the feet of Gamaliel in Jerusalem. Now on the whole, so far as we can tell (and it is only fair to warn you that there are some steps missing in the argument here), it was expected that a would-be Rabbi should be married, for obvious reasons of avoiding scandal. And although (as we have seen) Paul lets us hear of a good many criticisms levelled against him, the allegation that he was unmarried is never mentioned.

So *a priori* we might expect him to be married; and if that is so, it is hardly to be wondered at if his wife baulked at the idea of joining Paul on his dangerous and unceasing travelling. And if she were to be left anywhere, then Philippi, up there at the top end of Greece, clearly one of Paul's favourite communities, might have been a good place for her to stay and contribute to the local church. Philippi was a place that Paul could often visit, not far from the nearest port of Neapolis and with the excellent Roman road, the Via Egnatia, linking the two cities.

So it may be that Paul, far from being a misogynist, was in fact happily married, though often separated from his wife by the demands of his apostolic mission of telling the Gentiles about Jesus. The evidence is circumstantial and depends a good deal on speculation; but it is not negligible.

The fundamental equality of men and women

At all events, there is no indication in Paul that he retreats from his sense that all human beings, of whatever race, culture or religion, of whatever social class, or whatever gender, are equal 'in the Lord'. Even in 1 Corinthians, where, as we have seen, he might have had reason to restrain his teaching on the equality of men and women, he makes this clear. Look at 7:3–5, speaking of marriage (and so for 'woman' we might equally read 'wife', and for 'man', 'husband'):

> Let the man give to the woman what is her
> due; and likewise the woman to the man.
> The woman does not have authority over
> her own body, but the man does. Likewise,
> the man does not have authority over his
> own body, but the woman does.
> Don't deprive one another,
> except by agreement, for a time,
> in order to have leisure for prayer,
> and then come back together again . . .

Paul is here clearly convinced of the equality of husband and wife; and we have already seen how he asserts the liturgical equality of men and women when it comes to praying and prophesying (1 Corinthians 11:4–6); and more generally (1 Corinthians 11:11), with the telling qualifier 'in the Lord'.

Conclusion: what about those terrible 'household codes'?

A friend of mine, an eminent biblical scholar, finds the household codes quite intolerable; God cannot be speaking in them. Let us look, unafraid, at what the author (whether Paul or not) actually says.

The first passage, which we know already, is at Colossians 3:18–4:1:

> Wives, be subordinated to your husbands,
> as is fitting **in the Lord**. Husbands, love
> your wives, and don't get bitter against

> them. Children, obey your parents in every respect, for this is pleasing **in the Lord**. Parents, don't irritate your children, or they may get discouraged. Slaves, obey in every respect those who are your 'lords' according to the flesh, not as 'eye-slaves' or 'human-pleasers', but in simplicity of heart, **fearing the Lord**. Whatever you do, work at it from the heart, as **for the Lord**, and not for human beings, knowing that you will receive the reward of your inheritance **from the Lord**. Be **slaves of the Lord Christ**. For the one who does wrong will get the reward of the wrong they have done, and there is no respecting of status. 'Lords', give your slaves what is just and equitable, knowing that you also have a **Lord in heaven**.

Notice once again how Paul subverts the apparent insistence on the inferiority of wives, children, and slaves, in two ways. First, just as the apparently superior half of the pair is settling into complacency at having his status confirmed, a nudge in the ribs reminds him of equality. Second, notice the number of times in this passage when the Lord (printed in bold type) is mentioned, and how that undermines any notion that human beings can be superior to one another. It works, as we saw in the previous chapter, particularly effectively for the slave owners who are 'lords', but not the real thing, and who have to give an account. If that is so for slaves, then, even more, is it true for women; Paul cannot on the basis of this passage be twisted into service by those who wish to 'put women in their place'.

And let us look again at Ephesians 5:21–30, 32–33, clearly connected with the above passage, but longer than it:

> ... being **subordinated** to each other in reverence for Christ, the wives to their own husbands, as Christ is also the head of the church; he is the saviour of the body. But as the church is **subordinated** to Christ, so [should the wives be] to their husbands in every respect. Husbands, love your wives, as Christ also loved the church, and gave himself up on her behalf, in order that he might sanctify her, purifying her with a washing of water with a word in order to present the church to himself as radiant, having no spot or wrinkle. That is how husbands ought to love their own wives, like their own bodies. The one who loves his own wife loves himself, for no one ever hated his own flesh, but feeds it and nurtures it, just as Christ does with the church, for we are limbs of his body ... This is a great mystery; but I am speaking with regard to Christ and the church.

> But every single one of you must love your
> own wives as yourselves; and the wives
> should reverence their husbands.

This is a slightly more difficult passage; it seems to inscribe the inferiority of women to men, but it is worth noticing two things. Firstly, in that world, a husband who took these lines seriously would be very remarkable indeed, loving his wife as himself. Secondly, it seems, underneath it all, that Paul is really speaking of the relationship of Christ to the Church, and employing that important word 'mystery', which in Ephesians refers to God's astonishing plan. And in this context it is worth noticing that the passage both begins and ends with 'reverence' (or 'fear'), for Christ at the outset, and for the relationship of wife to husband at the end. You will have to make up your own mind whether to acquit our author of selling women short. Always, however, remember that it was Paul who wrote these astonishing lines (1 Corinthians 12:31–13:13), trying (unsuccessfully, alas) to persuade the Corinthians to put away their quarrels. As you read them, ask if the author of these words could possibly have put women into an inferior place in the church:

> Seek for the higher gifts; and I am showing
> you a way beyond parallel: if I speak in the
> languages of human beings and of angels,
> but do not have love, I have become an
> echoing bronze, or a clashing cymbal. And

if I have [the gift of] prophecy, and I know
all the mysteries, and all knowledge, and if I
have all faith, so as to shift mountains, but
do not have love, I am nothing. And if I
give away my possessions, bit by bit, and if
I give away my body in order to boast, but
do not have love, I am in no way helped.
Love is patient, and kindly; love is not
jealous, does not bear a grudge, is not
puffed up, does not behave indecently, does
not seek its own interests, is not provoked
to anger, does not count up wrongs, does
not rejoice at injustice, but instead rejoices
with the truth. Love bears all things,
believes all things, hopes all things,
endures all things. Love never fails.
As for prophecies, they will be cancelled
out; as for tongues, they will cease;
as for knowledge, it will be cancelled out.
For we know only partially, and we prophesy
only partially. When I was an infant, I spoke
like an infant, and had the mindset of an
infant, counted up like an infant. But when
I became an adult, I cancelled out infants'
things. For at present we see through a
looking-glass, obscurely. Then [we shall see]
face to face. At present, I know only partially.
Then I shall know just as I am known. So
there remain, faith, hope, love, these three
things. The greatest of these is love.

NOT THAT MAN!

Do you think that Paul is against women?
Do you think that all men and women are equal before God?
Do you think that Paul might have been married?
If so, are there any implications for today?

Twelve

Paul and sex

Introduction

The issues that sometimes come up under this heading, and which I shall try to consider in this chapter, are questions like, 'Is sex dirty?', (or 'is that what the Church thinks, and is it all Paul's fault?'). It has to be admitted that the Church is not always its own best friend in this regard, and can sometimes give the (false) impression of being unhealthily interested in what goes on in people's bedrooms, and nothing else. When it comes to Paul on sex, it has to be said that on all sides of the various debates that go on in our world, there is a tendency, at least among those who read the Bible, for everybody to claim Paul as an ally, answering questions that had very probably never occurred to him. So we must tread carefully, for that reason, and because sex is (if a committed celibate may be permitted to offer this comment) enormously important.

We should also notice, as a fact about the world in which we live, that it does not take very much notice of what Christians say about matters of sexual morality; and this includes a good many young people who regard themselves as Christians in good standing. We can respond in one of two ways, both of them wrong if taken too far. We can robustly assert, 'Well, they are wrong, and they must listen to us.' Or we can, rather more timidly, mutter 'They are quite right, of course, and we must listen to them.' We can, I think, steer between these extremes; but let us concentrate on St Paul, and whether he has anything to say to us today.

Paul was a well-brought up Jew

We have to remember, all the time, that Paul was brought up as a traditionally minded Jew, a decidedly enthusiastic Pharisee, for whom sex was something too important to be done outside marriage. In that respect Paul was no different from Christians whose education took place more than a generation ago, in most cultures. To say that is neither to criticise Paul, nor to commend him, but to state a fact. If I may for this purpose lift my head above the parapet, I should also say that I have yet to be convinced that what in the 1960s was called 'sexual liberation' has in fact increased the sum of human happiness, even though I recognise that it may well be impossible to turn the clock back; but I have seen too many young people wounded by their experiences to be convinced that it is appropriate to express oneself sexually as and when one pleases. Paul, I think, would have shared that view, and certainly found himself shocked by what passed for conventional sexual morality in a place like Corinth. It is against that background that we must see Paul's understanding of sexual morality, in all the issues that follow.

What about homosexuality?

Paul, I think there is no doubt, would have accepted the standard Jewish condemnation of homosexual intercourse, and of what went on in that respect in contemporary Greek society. When in the first chapter of Romans he lists the elements of the mess into which Gentiles have got themselves, his Jewish hearers would probably have applauded, especially when they heard the following lines:

> Because of this, God gave them up to
> dishonourable feelings; for their women
> changed their natural intercourse for
> unnatural intercourse, and, likewise, their
> men abandoned the natural form of
> intercourse, with women, and they burnt
> with desire for each other, males
> committing indecency on males, and
> receiving the inevitable penalty in
> themselves for their aberration. And
> because they did not see fit to keep God
> on their intellectual horizon, God gave
> them over to an unfitting intellect,
> to do things that are unfitting . . .
>
> *Romans 1:26–28*

It is impossible to conjure out of these lines a Paul who is in favour of homosexual activity. Paul would simply have accepted the tenets of his Jewish background on this issue. We need, however, to be aware of his rhetorical purpose here. What he does in chapter one of Romans is to get his Jewish hearers to nod their heads complacently as they hear the list of things that the Gentiles have got wrong, only for Paul then to turn sharply on them at 2:1. And consider the list that Paul offers at 1 Corinthians 6:9–10:

> Or do you not realise that the unjust shall not inherit the kingdom of God? Don't be led astray: neither fornicators nor idolaters nor catamites nor sodomites, nor thieves, nor drunkards, nor those who utter abuse, nor pirates (!), shall inherit the kingdom of God.

Here Paul is just producing a list, a whole range of negative terms, to indicate that a certain level of behaviour is expected of those who are 'in Christ'. So we are not to take this list as the result of a carefully thought-out argument. Paul simply assumed that as regards this list, he and the Corinthians were in agreement, even though he could also say (verse 11) that 'some of you were these things'. Perhaps therefore we should not read the list as 'behaviour to avoid' so much as 'activities in which you were imprisoned, and from which Christ has set you free'. I suspect that homosexual activity would have seemed to Paul as pure self-indulgence on the part of these disoriented Gentiles, something that no one in their right mind could possibly naturally aspire to, and also as part of the mess to which they were sentenced, and from which God liberated them in Christ.

Does what Paul says about homosexuality solve a problem of our day? Probably not; it is unlikely that he would have been aware that there are people who are homosexual, and who have no sense of a calling to celibacy. If he had known that, he would have had to do some intense theological thinking, and we have already seen that he is very good at that. What his answer would have been we are not in a position to say. Some today affirm stoutly that he would have been against all homosexual activity, even under those circumstances; others again take a different view.

What about incest?

People sometimes say, just a bit too casually, that incest is not a particularly prominent difficulty in the Church today; but actually, that is not quite true. Most cases of child abuse take place within the family, and many pastors have had to deal with some of the difficulties. Paul would have known (and strongly disapproved of) the practice among the Ptolemy dynasty in Egypt, of sisters marrying their brothers. And he had this to say of a case of incest in Corinth:

> It is actually reported that there is sexual immorality among you, and sexual immorality of a kind that is not even [known] among the Gentiles, that someone has his father's wife! And you people are 'puffed up'; shouldn't you rather be in

mourning, that the one who has committed
his crime should be plucked out from your
midst?

1 Corinthians 5:1–2

In verses 3–5 Paul then passes sentence on the person in absentia:

to hand over such a one to Satan for the
destruction of the flesh, that the spirit may
be rescued on the Lord's Day.

Finally in verses 6–8, he reveals his basic argument:

Your boast is not good. Don't you realise
that a little leaven leavens the entire lump
of dough? Clean up your act and get the
old leaven out, so that you can be new
dough, as you are unleavened loaves.
For Christ our Passover has been sacrificed.
So let us celebrate the festival, not in the
old leaven, nor in the leaven of evil and
wickedness, but in the unleavened bread of
sincerity and truth.

The point here is that incest has an effect on the entire body of Christ (a very important doctrine in this letter, as we have seen). That is why Paul is so strongly against sexual immorality. The frequently reiterated claim that 'we weren't hurting anybody' would not cut much ice with Paul.

One other thing to notice is the reference to Passover, the Feast of Unleavened Bread. It is quite likely that Paul was writing this letter at the time of this greatest of all Jewish festivals, which was also, of course, the time when Jesus died and was raised; so also in his mind is a certain horror at the pollution of what ought to be very holy indeed.

Fornication

The Greek word for 'fornication' is *porneia*, which means all kinds of sexual immorality, but especially having recourse to prostitutes. The Greek word for a prostitute is *porne*, and you can see the connection with the English word 'pornography'. Whatever it is, Paul will have none of it. It was (or was said to be) a particular problem in Corinth, a city that (like many towns with a harbour attached) had a certain reputation in that regard, so much so that the Greek verb *korinthiazomai* means, in the decorous language of the dictionary, 'to practice whoredom'. And the Roman historian Plutarch reports a legend, one that may be a libel on the city, that at the Temple of Aphrodite (goddess of sexual love) in the city there were a thousand ritual prostitutes who would assist devotees in their religious practice in this regard. Even if that is not true, the Christians in Corinth seem to have walked rather uncertainly on this matter, and Paul found that he had to address them in these uncompromising terms (1 Corinthians 6:15–20):

> ... don't you know that your bodies are Christ's limbs? So am I going to take Christ's limbs and turn them into limbs of a prostitute? No way! Don't you realise that the person who sticks to a prostitute is one *body* with her? You see, [Scripture] says, 'the two shall become one flesh'. But the one who sticks to the Lord is one *spirit* [with him]. Avoid fornication: every other kind of sin that a person commits is outside the body; but the one who fornicates, sins against his own body. Or don't you realise that your [plural] body is the Temple among you of the Holy Spirit, which you have from God – and you do not belong to yourselves? You were bought at a price. So glorify God in your [plural] body.

Notice how the idea of 'body' runs through the argument here, as indeed it does throughout the whole letter; but it is a slightly blurred notion. At the beginning, the sense of 'body' is clearly that which has sexual intercourse; but then we hear of Christ's limbs, and we are talking about the body of Christ, which is 'the Church' in this letter. Then, however, the meaning apparently reverts to the-body-which-fornicates. But back it comes at the end, and the 'body of you [plural]' has to be once more the Church. At all events, Paul has no patience with any idea that sexual misbehaviour is compatible with membership of the Body of Christ.

So much is this the case that elsewhere in the Pauline corpus 'fornication' is not even to be mentioned:

> Fornication and impurity of all kinds, and greed should not even be named among you, as is appropriate to the saints, and [likewise] ugly behaviour, foolish conversation or buffoonery, which are unfitting; rather there should be thanksgiving. Be sure of this, that no fornicator or impure or greedy person (that's idolatry), has any share in the kingdom of Christ and God.
>
> *Ephesians 5:3–5*

This is another of those lists, and you might argue that Paul is just reaching for any kind of negative term; but notice that he mentions 'fornication' twice here, and notice also how, characteristically, he ends with 'Christ and God', which is the context of all his thinking about how Christians should behave.

Here is another, very similar, list, from Colossians 3:5:

> So put to death those limbs that are on earth: fornication, impurity, passion, evil desire, and the greed that is [really] idolatry.

And compare the certainty that Paul shows in 1 Thessalonians 4:3–7:

> For this is God's will – your holiness, for you to steer clear from fornication, for each of you to know how to keep his vessel in holiness and honour, not in passionate desire, like the Gentiles who do not know God, not to transgress and to desire your brother, because the Lord avenges all these things, just as we told you before, and we solemnly testify now. For God did not call us to impurity, but to holiness.

For completeness, we add the list that is to be found in 1 Timothy 1:9–10:

> ... knowing this, that the Law does not lie heavy on those who use it lawfully, but on the lawless and the insubordinate, the impious and sinful, the unholy and profane, patricides and matricides and homicides, fornicators, sodomites, kidnappers, liars, perjurers, and anything else that is opposed to healthy teaching ...

It seems a slightly uneven list, this; but once again we see Paul's conviction that there are forms of behaviour that are incompatible with being 'in Christ'. Not just anything will do, and sexual behaviour matters.

On the other hand, we cannot stress too often that Paul would not have expected us to be reading his letters today. He is writing to churches whose situation and problems he knows quite well; and before he would write to our churches, he would have to find out a good deal more about our situation. But we can be sure that on matters of sex he would not offer us carte blanche, whatever the current ethos of our culture may say.

Marriage is good

Paul is not, however, opposed to all sexual self-expression. He knows of the importance of marriage. The place to look for evidence here is 1 Corinthians 7, especially verses 1–2:

> Now, about what you wrote, 'it is good for
> a man not to touch a woman'. But because
> of fornications, each man should have his
> own woman, and each woman her own man.

Two things need to be said here. First is that only now is Paul condescending to answer their rather complacent letter to him (and we can be sure that this is quite deliberate). Second, 'it is good for a man not to touch a woman' is almost certainly, in the judgement of scholars, not Paul's teaching but the slogan of an ascetic group in Corinth, who *were* arguing that 'sex is dirty', and whom Paul was opposing.

Now it is true that we may raise an eyebrow at his suggestion that marriage is valuable only because people need to be able to do something with the sexual desires that they experience. The point is that he regards it as a good thing, in a world where attitudes to marriage were somewhat ambiguous; and within marriage, as we have seen, he regards men and women as equal, and as having equal rights to sexual intercourse.

Paul can sound a bit negative

It is true that sometimes Paul sounds a note that gives a rather stark view of marriage and sex, and that we in the Church have sometimes followed what we take to be his lead. So in the same chapter (7:9) Paul addresses the 'unmarried and the widows', and tells them that:

> if they cannot remain chaste, let them
> get married, for it is better to marry than
> to burn.

Whether 'burning' in this verse refers to burning with lust or (at a later date) burning in Hell, it is hard to turn the sentiment into any very positive view of marriage. Nevertheless, Paul can teach our age, if only we shall listen, of the importance of sex, and of getting it right. He is clear that marriage is for life (7:11), but also knows that some marriages can come to an end (7:15). Once again, we have to emphasise that he is giving advice to the Christians in Corinth in his century and not to Christians all over the world in ours. The fact is that we need a certain humility here, for we do not know enough to be sure what Paul would say to us today.

What about Christians today?

All too often, Christians can sound extraordinarily condemnatory of other people's failings. It is essential that we should sound a positive note, like Jesus and (at his best) Paul. It is also important that we recognise that sex matters, and that we trivialise it if we say that 'anything goes'.

How are we to resolve the problems that face us today about sexual morality? Not, it is clear, simply by quoting a line from St Paul as though that could end the matter. The context of our decisions must, however, *always* be the context of Paul's decisions, namely the old story of God, and the new story of Christ.

Did Paul think that sex was 'dirty'?
Is Paul's teaching on sex helpful to us today?

Conclusion

This book will have done what it set out to do if, after struggling through to the end, you find yourself persuaded to have another look at Paul; and if you feel that after all he is not quite as dangerous as you might have supposed; if you have realised that, after all, you do not 'hate' the Apostle to the Gentiles.

Is there anything else to say here? Perhaps. In the opening lines of what may be Paul's earliest letter, and the first surviving document of the entire New Testament, you will read of:

> ... your work of faith, and your labour of love, and your endurance of hope in our Lord Jesus Christ, in the presence of our God and Father ...
> *1 Thessalonians 1:3*

There are two points to notice here. First, look at how Paul insists on the context: his beloved Jesus, to whom he gives the title of 'Lord', which as we have seen makes a very lofty claim, and the name of 'Messiah', the one sent by God; and 'God and Father' is the other part of that context. So Paul still regards his message as telling the ancient story of God and the people of God, the narrative in which he was brought up, in Tarsus and Jerusalem. And the story of God must from now on include the astonishing fact that God raised Jesus from the dead.

Second, Paul notices that this fact evokes certain responses from those who are in Christ. Here he expresses these responses in terms of 'faith, love, and hope'; in 1 Corinthians 13:13, trying to persuade the Corinthians to stop fighting, he mentions the same triad again, after drawing the portrait of his beloved Jesus, 'As it is, there remain faith, hope, love, these three things. And the greatest of these is love.'

These two points take us right to the heart of St Paul, and we shall do well to reflect on them, and to try to live them out.

Do you 'hate' St Paul? If so, why?
What do you think has been his influence down the
   ages? Has it been bad, or good?
Will you go back to read Paul after this?

Suggestions for further reading

Books marked * are very good but heavy going, not to be attempted by beginners!

Barnett, Paul (2008) *Paul: Missionary of Jesus*, Eerdmans.

Byrne, Brendan SJ (1996): *Romans* (Sacra Pagina series), Liturgical Press.

Cantalamessa, Raniero (2002) *Life in Christ: A Spiritual Commentary on the Letter to the Romans*, Protea Book House, Pretoria.

Dunn, James G., ed. (2003) *The Cambridge Companion to St Paul*, Cambridge University Press.

Dunn, James G., ed. (2003) *The Theology of Paul the Apostle*,* second edition, T & T Clark.

Fee, Gordon D. (2007) *Pauline Christology*,* Hendrickson.

Fitzmyer, Joseph A., SJ (1993) *Romans* (Anchor Bible Series).

Fitzmyer, Joseph A., SJ (2000) *Philemon* (Anchor Bible Series).

Grieb, A. Katherine (2002) *The Story of Romans*,* Westminster John Knox Press.

Harrington, Daniel J., SJ (2008) *Meeting St Paul Today*, Loyola Press.

Hays, Richard B. (2005) *The Conversion of the Imagination: Paul as Interpreter of Israel's Scriptures*, Eerdmans.

Hengel, Martin, and Schwemer Anna Maria (1997), *Paul Between Damascus and Antioch – The Unknown Years*,* Westminster John Knox Press.

Hooker, Morna D. (2004) *Paul: A Short Introduction*, One World.

Horrell, David G. (2006) *An Introduction to the Study of Paul*, second edition, T & T Clark.

Murphy-O'Connor, Jerome OP (1995) *Paul the Letter-Writer: His World, His Options, His Skills*, Michael Glazier.

Murphy-O'Connor, Jerome (2004) *Paul, His Story*, Oxford University Press.

Murphy-O'Connor, Jerome (2002) *St Paul's Corinth: Text and Archaeology*, second edition.

Sanders, E. P. (1977) *Paul and Palestinian Judaism*,* SCM Press.

Sanders, E. P. (2001) *Paul: A Very Short Introduction*, Oxford University Press.

Theissen, Gerd (1982) *The Social Setting of Pauline Christianity: Essays on Corinth*,* Fortress Press.

Thisleton, Anthony C. (2000) *The First Epistle to the Corinthians*,* New International Greek Testament Commentary, Eerdmans.

Wenham, David (1995) *Paul: Follower of Jesus or Founder of Christianity?* * Eerdmans.

Wright, N.T. (1997) *What St Paul Really Said*, Eerdmans.

Wright, N.T. (2005) *Paul: Fresh Perspectives*, SPCK.

Ziesler, John (1983) *Pauline Christianity*, Oxford University Press.

www.ingramcontent.com/pod-product-compliance
Lightning Source LLC
Chambersburg PA
CBHW020403080526
44584CB00014B/1149